The Agile Manager's Guide To

MANAGING CHANGE

The Agile Manager's Guide To

MANAGING CHANGE

By Robert J. Ristino

Velocity Business Publishing
Bristol, Vermont USA

Velocity Business Publishing publishes authoritative works of the highest quality. It is not, however, in the business of offering professional, legal, or accounting advice. Each company has its own circumstances and needs, and state and national laws may differ with respect to issues affecting you. If you need legal or other advice pertaining to your situation, secure the services of a professional.

Copyright © 2000 by Robert J. Ristino
Second printing, March 2001
All Rights Reserved
Printed in the United States of America
Library of Congress Catalog Card Number 00-102365
ISBN 1-58099-019-3
Title page illustration by Elayne Sears

Printed in Canada

If you'd like additional copies of this book or a catalog of books in the Agile Manager Series®, please get in touch.

- **Write us:**
  Velocity Business Publishing, Inc.
  15 Main Street
  Bristol, VT 05443 USA

- **Call us:**
  1-888-805-8600 in North America (toll-free)
  1-802-453-6669 from all other countries

- **Fax us:**
  1-802-453-2164

- **E-mail us:**
  action@agilemanager.com

- **Visit our Web site:**
  www.agilemanager.com

The Web site contains much of interest to business people—tips and techniques, business news, links to valuable sites, and electronic versions of titles in the Agile Manager Series.

To get in touch with Robert J. Ristino, call 508-429-5530 or visit www.ristinopeters.com

*To my wife Mary and daughters Laurie and Gaelin,
who have successfully managed to change me*

Contents

Books in the Agile Manager Series®:

Chapter One

Understand
The Nature of Change

"Big happening," said the Agile Manager as he passed Wanda in the hall. "It looks like we may be merging with Murphy Technology."

"Wait!" she said as he sailed by her briskly.

"I can't," he said, half turning around. "I'm late for a meeting about it. And by the way—don't tell anyone yet."

Wanda stood motionless in the hallway for a full thirty seconds as she let the news sink in. As second-in-command in the product development department, she knew she'd have a counterpart at Murphy. Her mind raced: Would they both keep their jobs? Could she get more responsibility? Would she lose her job? Would they double the size of the department? Would they close one of the companies entirely? Would they . . .

"Things change," remarks actor Don Ameche in the movie by the same name, when the aging Italian immigrant he plays wins, then loses, a small fortune gambling.

Ameche's sage comment reflects an understanding of the transient nature of both luck and life. Wait and they'll soon change.

Change is endemic to life. It is both constant and necessary.

"Change teaches," writes Robert Grudin, "that we are part of an evolving order, a cycle of birth, growth, fruition, and decay that requires (but also transcends) our participation as individuals."

In fact, rather than destroying order and stability, change is in itself a form of order. Without change, entropy would occur. That means systems would run down into disorganized states.

Change is, in effect, essential for life. Without it we become stale, impoverished. Change rejuvenates us, as well as the organizations we toil in and for. Bottom line: change or perish. It's as simple as that.

Best Tip

Change or perish. But understand that change is good. It rejuvenates us—as well as the companies we work for.

Does that mean you have to love it? Of course not. That's like saying you should love stress. But, then again, stress can be helpful. It can give you that edge—that little extra juice that separates exceptional performance from good performance.

Change helps in much the same way. It provides new perspectives, new opportunities, and new challenges. And change provides new learning experiences that can pay huge dividends as you move up the management ladder.

So let's not fear change. Let's embrace it!

Easiest to Deal With: Routine Change

So we can look at change as essential—the energy of organizational life. Of course, I wouldn't want to say that to someone about to lose his or her job because of change. In most cases, though, change is neither frightening, unusual, nor cause for someone losing a job. Most change is, in fact, routine. We all experience it.

In organizations, we experience routine change as operational fine-tuning. These are changes in personnel policies, sales strategy, shift schedules, a production line, products, and management—ordinary, everyday changes we all live with at work.

Such changes, incidentally, can create problems if not handled properly. But, for the most part, organizations and those they employ have become rather elegant in planning and implementing routine change. As we'll see in chapter three, these planning skills can also help you manage other kinds of change as well.

Scarier: Nonroutine Change

Less elegant, however, is how organizations handle other kinds of change. Change is not static. It moves along a continuum. On one end is routine change. On the other is nonroutine change, which causes organizations the most trouble. It includes the radical, anxiety-producing change that comes from downsizing (you have to love that euphemism), rightsizing (a misnomer if ever there was one), mergers, closures, acquisitions, affiliations, and—an all-time favorite—reengineering.

|Best Tip

Know that all employees facing a change of any magnitude will be thinking, 'What about me?'

Much of this book is about managing nonroutine change. But the skills you learn will serve you well in handling change of any magnitude.

Nonroutine Change Causes Resistance

Nonroutine, or radical, change presents the greatest challenge to you and your organization. That's because it causes the most resistance among employees, managers included.

Why? I'll identify a number of reasons as we proceed. But understand for now that, more often than not, employees resist change because they are afraid of losing their jobs. They see radical change as very threatening. It is fear of the unknown.

Ultimately, all change comes to be seen by employees as a WAM (What about me?) issue: "How will this change affect me either personally or professionally?" It's the most basic and natural question to ask. It is one you'll ask yourself when change happens.

If you don't make a compelling case for change (something this book will help you do), you can expect resistance. Sometimes it's strong enough to ruin the change effort.

Expect Organizational Anxiety

Radical change has the potential to cause fear because it produces anxiety. Organizational anxiety results from the uncertainty that surrounds change.

Organizational-development experts tell us that uncertainty arises from the difference between information available and information needed. Stated more simply, that is the difference between what people want to know and what you tell them. In short, the answer to those WAM questions. The greater the gap between these two variables, the greater the anxiety among employees and the greater the degree of resistance to change.

Unfortunately, radical change often produces large gaps between what people need to know and what they actually know. This gap has two causes. The first is management's failure to communicate effectively on issues of concern to employees. The second consists of information gaps inherent in the process of nonroutine change itself. These gaps include:

Make a compelling case for change, or you can expect resistance.

- The scarcity of reliable information due to the unpredictable effects of change that will occur in the distant future.
- Management's desire to guard sensitive information associated with nonroutine change—because such change is invariably strategic in nature.
- The withholding of information due to management's fear that releasing it may raise rather than lower anxiety.

One major pitfall with sharing information is that the accuracy of such information is often marginal at best. Information about radical change is usually based on best-guess scenarios or the best thinking available by those planning the major change.

For example, employees involved in a merger are going to want to know what part of the organization is moving, consolidating, or reorganizing. The truth often is: No one knows for sure. That's because the change will occur sometime in the future.

Unlike Johnny Carson's inscrutable soothsayer, Karnak the Magnificent, who would announce the question when given the answer, management has a more difficult task. It must predict the answers to as-yet unasked questions.

Best Tip

To help minimize organizational anxiety, resist the urge to share more information than is necessary.

To avoid or minimize information problems, it's important to think through your communications strategy, something I'll help you do in chapter four.

Understand Organizational Responses to Change

Like people, organizations have different approaches to adapting to change. You've probably experienced some if not all of these adaptive behaviors at work. Some are constructive, others not.

Moreover, the manner in which the organization deals with change is not necessarily uniform throughout. Units, departments, and divisions may have very different approaches to dealing with the imposed change depending on a number of variables.

These differing behaviors often reflect the manager's response to change. A fearful manager, for instance, creates a fearful workforce.

Adaptive behaviors, both good and bad, are influenced by the following factors:

- Extent of the imposed change: Does it involve every part of the organization or only one or a few units?
- Duration of the change initiative: Will it take days, weeks,

months, or years to implement?
- Who bears the brunt: Is the organizational unit in the middle of the change or peripheral to it? If peripheral, how will the change impact the unit?
- Strength of the impact: What will be the extent of that impact? Deeply felt, or superficial?
- Perceived value: Is the impact considered negative or positive?

The answers to these questions provide insight into how particular units may respond to the change.

Here are some of the more common responses to change that you may have experienced with other managers and their employees:

- Championing
- Cooperating
- Tolerating
- Avoiding
- Obfuscating
- Dismissing
- Attacking
- Co-opting

Championing. Manager and unit are heavily involved in the change. They are true believers. They are apostles carrying the word forth throughout the organization. They are role models for change in the company.

Such behavior often occurs when implementing total quality management or reengineering initiatives. *"We're really excited about this new just-in-time inventory system. It's going to dramatically increase profitability, decrease delivery times, and improve customer service."*

Cooperating. Those affected actively support and enable the change to be implemented. Active or passive advocacy for the change initiative also shows evidence of cooperation: *"We'll do whatever we can to help you implement the new inventory system. Just let us know how we can help."*

Tolerating. People are neutral on the change initiative. They do not obstruct it, but neither are they proactive in supporting it or enabling it to occur. To them, the change is a nuisance, like a chronic backache, to be borne with managerial stoicism. *"Good luck with implementing that new system. I'm glad it's your baby and not mine."*

Avoiding. People passively resist implementing the change. This often occurs when people feel threatened by the change but are unable to confront management openly on the issue. They create a variety of reasons for not doing what must be done to move forward with the change initiative. *"We'll try to get those inventory figures to you as soon as possible, but you know how things are. Everybody wants everything yesterday. Talk to you later."*

Best **T**ip
Keep your chin up at all times. A fearful manager creates a fearful workforce.

Obfuscating. This is a more sophisticated approach to delaying the change. Managers identify various issues, concerns, or other operational imperatives for preventing their active support or involvement in the change initiative. *"We'd like to help, but I've just finished installing this new computer system. Integrating the new inventory software into our MIS system may take a while."*

Dismissing. People dismiss the change initiative out of hand. Without vested interest in the change, managers dismiss it as counterproductive and a waste of their time and energy to be involved. *"I don't see any benefit to the organization with this new inventory system. I think our efforts could be better spent in other areas."*

Attacking. Out and out opposition. Managers and staff publicly criticize and/or condemn the change initiative. *"Dumbest thing I've ever heard of. They're wasting a lot of time and money putting in new tracking and inventory systems. It won't save a dime! They're just doing it to cut more jobs."*

Co-opting. The change initiative is subsumed under the umbrella of another activity of more interest and/or concern to the manager. *"Don't worry about our participation in the new inventory system. I have a new process coming on line that will do the same thing anyway."*

Sound familiar? Well, they are. We've all experienced these reactions whenever change is taking place in an organization. In general, organizational units respond to change with self-interest in mind. When they perceive the change as threatening, they respond accordingly.

> **Best Tip**
>
> Plan to help employees overcome the pain that comes from losing co-workers, supervisors, established routines, and responsibilities.

You'll also see some, if not all, of these behaviors reflected by your employees whenever you're implementing change in your department.

But fear not, because you'll soon learn many techniques for making sure you are surrounded by more champions and co-operators than avoiders and attackers.

Expect Stress and Feelings of Loss

Organizational responses simply reveal the attitudes and behaviors of managers and their employees. They may also reflect the attitudes and opinions of members of senior management. Often, radical change is implemented by the CEO without the total support of the leadership.

These attitudes and behaviors reflect the workplace stress and the workplace loss that both managers and employees experience while undergoing change.

Workplace Stress. The workplace naturally causes stress for a variety of reasons. They include poor work environments, increasing productivity demands, changes in duties and responsibilities, poor compensation and benefits, lack of recognition or appreciation, problems with co-workers and/or supervisors, and lack of opportunities for growth.

Radical change increases these stressors. Recent studies have shown that workplace stress associated with a radical change not only affects performance on the job, but also family life. Researchers studied a group of health-care workers under stress because of continuous downsizing in the health-care industry. They found that the stress health-care workers were experiencing on the job also caused problems at home.

Workplace Loss. One other major cause of stress is loss in the workplace. "Loss" covers a lot of territory. It can be an employee losing his or her job, a person's co-workers losing their jobs, changes in the work site, the dismissal or reassignment of a supervisor or manager, a reduction in compensation/benefits, or changes in roles and responsibilities. Any of these losses can affect an employee to some degree.

Employees experience one or more of these losses during a radical change, which is another reason why such change tends to be very disruptive to the organization and its workforce.

As you'll see in chapters five and six, managing a sense of loss among the workforce provides you with your greatest challenge. That's because you'll have to manage loss and other negative effects of change *while* you put the change plan into action. That's a juggling act that takes some skill.

Revitalize the Workforce through Change

Clearly, managing change can be a daunting task. But, if done right, it can both revitalize and challenge the workforce and the organization. Of course, knowing the right way to manage change isn't easy. That's why you're reading this book. I've lived through change both big and small and I've learned a lot along the way. I've written this book to share those lessons with you. So my pain is your gain. I'll show you how to manage change that will enhance your performance and the performance of those who work for and with you.

I'm sure you just can't wait to absorb the lessons I'm about to teach, but take my advice and first understand how good leadership can make change easier—the topic of the next chapter.

After that, we'll discuss the nuts and bolts of managing routine and nonroutine change, understanding and managing loss in the workplace, understanding and overcoming resistance to change, and handling the stress that inevitably comes with change.

The Agile Manager's Lessons Learned

✔ Understand that change is essential to life.
✔ Realize from the start that radical change—mergers, closures, downsizings, and acquisitions among them—is the most anxiety-producing form of organizational change.
✔ Expect both people and organizational units as a whole to respond to change with self-interest in mind.
✔ Be aware that employees can experience both stress and loss as a result of change in the workplace.

Chapter Two

The Manager's Role In Managing Change

As the Agile Manager sat at his desk with the massive report on the potential merger on his lap, his mind wandered back to a conversation about a merger he'd had about fifteen years ago with Dick Jonas, a great boss and his first real mentor.

"Why should we tell them anything?" said the Agile Manager. "Wouldn't it be better to keep them in the dark about what's happening?"

"Do you like to be kept in the dark?" asked Jonas. He waited for an answer.

"Well . . . no," said the Agile Manager.

"Why not?" Again Jonas waited.

"If I know something is going on, I have a lot of questions I want answered."

"Precisely," said Jonas. "And so do our people. If we don't share our vision and goals for this change, people will make up incredible stories about why we're doing it. And an organization can become paralyzed when wild-eyed rumors start bouncing around. Why, I remember . . ."

It's a heady role that you, as a manager, must play in managing change. In fact, the success of all change management rests squarely on your shoulders. It is you that employees interact with daily. It is you they look to for answers to their questions. It is you who they seek out for help and guidance. And it is you who more often than not has both their respect and trust.

In meeting these responsibilities you play many roles. You have to be first and foremost a leader. But you must also be an educator, a coach, a motivator, and a mentor. You must move among these roles simply, effortlessly, and with great agility. Not easy, but whoever told you it would be?

Best Tip

Polish your management skills. You need to be a good manager before you can become a good changemaster.

Before we look at each of these roles in detail, note that this chapter comprises a short primer on good management skills. It's important to cover this ground, because managers who can lead, educate, coach, motivate, and mentor will have the necessary skills to lead successful change initiatives.

If the fires of change are burning your feet right now, skip ahead to chapter three or four for immediate relief. But when things settle down, come back here. It will help you better manage the next change you face.

Lead

"The first responsibility of a leader is to define reality," writes Max DePree in his book *Leadership Is an Art.* "The last is to say thank you. In between the two, the leader must become a servant and a debtor. That sums up the progress of an artful leader."

The role of leader is by far the most difficult and critical. As a leader you must take risks. You must be willing to make decisions, quickly and decisively, and be willing to live with the consequences of those decisions. Moreover, you must do so while remaining calm and composed even though others lose their collective cool. You must have what the French call *sang froid.*

Translated simply it means *cold blood* or coolness under fire.
An agile leader does the following:

- Articulates the organization's vision.
- Creates and inspires the work team.
- Shares short and long-term goals.
- Determines direction.
- Fosters self-esteem.
- Accepts responsibility for failure, but shares success.

Articulate the organization's vision. Your employees should understand and be committed to the organization's vision for the future. This is especially true when an organization is undergoing radical change such as a merger. As you'll see in **chapter four**, communicating vision is the first step in managing radical change. Employees have to understand the nature of the change in the context of the organization's overall vision. Then the change is more easily understood and accepted. It is difficult to motivate employees to perform outstandingly when they lack commitment to a commonly held, overarching goal.

Management gurus James Collins and Jerry Porras call this a BHAG, a *Big, Hairy, Audacious Goal*. That could be, for example, Honda's desire to beat out GM as the world's number one auto maker or your company's commitment to doubling sales in one year. The goal doesn't matter. What matters is that your organization's vision of the future is shared with and understood by your employees. It is your responsibility to ensure that it is.

Create and inspire work teams. Work teams are not born. They are created. You are the creator. Whether you inherit or have hired most of your staff, they are yours. You are responsible for molding them into a cohesive work team that is dedicated to the success of the group.

That means:

- Understanding the strengths and weaknesses of each team member;
- Assigning tasks and responsibilities that correspond with

those strengths and weaknesses;

■ Ensuring that all your staff has the best chance of achieving individual success thereby contributing to the overall success of the work team.

Always play to people's strengths, and not their weaknesses. Avoid trying to turn a weakness into a strength. Rather, strive to compensate for that weakness by enhancing individual strengths.

A few years ago I had an employee who had a marvelous creative flair. Unfortunately, she wasn't detail oriented. While her projects were imaginative and well received by her clients, some would run into problems because the devil is always in the details. Naturally, one or more of my staff would have to come to her rescue. While this irritated some, they understood and accepted her limitations, knowing that her positive contributions to our team success far outweighed the negatives.

We recognized that you can't put a square peg in a round hole. Instead, you look for a square hole. What she did, she did very well. She was like a good wing in hockey who could pot a goal when you needed it but was hopeless playing defense. So we would play "D" while she did her thing. That way we all won.

You'll also inspire your people by demonstrating positive work habits, showing your commitment to the team, recognizing good performance, and encouraging outstanding performance by providing the team with interesting and challenging work.

By keeping people challenged during periods of change, they will continue to feel they are a vital and important part of the organization and its change initiatives.

Share short- and long-term goals. One effective method for dealing with the effects of radical change is to keep your employees' collective eyes on the prize. Ensure that they all know what your unit's short- and long-term goals are. These can be quantitative, such as production or sales goals. Or they can be qualitative, such as goals associated with a change initiative like continuous quality improvement.

When practical, also involve employees in developing implementation plans. You will find that joint planning can be a very powerful tool in managing change.

Determine direction. With agreed-upon short- and long-term goals and objectives, you provide direction to your team on how to accomplish them. You keep people focused on the job at hand, which is especially necessary during periods of radical change.

Emphasize taking immediate action steps and accomplishing short-term goals. Teach them to prioritize work and allocate resources based on accomplishing those goals. Keep them focused on the plan.

Best Tip

Keep people focused on goals, especially during periods of radical change.

Foster self-esteem. Probably your most powerful motivational tool is your ability to raise an employee's self-esteem. Too often, managers see themselves as disciplinarians—as task masters rather than task enablers.

Seek out opportunities to make people feel good about themselves. I don't mean for you to be artificial or self-serving. However, you'll find many genuine opportunities to praise people. Identify and take advantage of them.

When praising, do so in public. When criticizing, do so in private. And all criticism should be constructive. Also, a small "thank you" can be just as powerful as public praise. The small courtesies you pay people during the day have a cumulative, positive effect. That's why saying "thank you" is one of the leader's primary tasks.

Take responsibility for failure, but share success. The leader does not blame or discipline employees for failure—or allow anyone else to do so. And in success, the leader always ensures that as many as possible share in the praise for that success.

Both employees and management respect the leader who accepts total responsibility for failure. Employees will respect you for protecting them from blame and shame. Management will respect you for being ready to assume responsibility for your actions and those of your employees. You will be a manager that others will want to work with and for.

General Robert E. Lee was such a leader. After Picket's disastrous charge at Gettysburg, Lee confronted his retreating troops and begged forgiveness for ordering the doomed attack. He told them the failure was his, not theirs. They would not hear it. Typical of his leadership style, the incident served only to add to Lee's stature among his troops.

Educate

In articulating the organization's vision and providing direction for the work team, you must continuously educate the workforce about the competitive marketplace.

Best Tip
Take the time to educate your people about the competitive marketplace. If you do, they'll adapt to change better.

Your boss often asks you to convey to your staff news about a change in the organization, sometimes good, sometimes bad. It could be an announcement about a new CEO, divestiture of a product line, a major layoff, or a merger or acquisition.

While such news should be shared, it must be shared with some explanation. Employees must be able to understand the event as it applies to the future success of the organization and the impact, if any, it will have on them personally.

Moreover, the need for change, especially radical change, is made more credible when the necessity for such change is understood by all.

You, as educator, are responsible for ensuring that employees understand:

- The competitive marketplace.
- The organization's strategic and marketing plans and objectives.

- The organization's business performance.
- The team's performance.

The competitive marketplace. It amazes me that managers believe employees are neither interested nor concerned about what is happening outside their four walls. We assume too much. And even when there is little or no interest, it is still your responsibility to educate employees about the realities of the marketplace.

A general understanding of the competitive marketplace gives employees a better appreciation for the problems and issues that your company must face to be successful. It provides the necessary background for understanding strategic actions like merging, downsizing, or acquiring another company. It also helps employees make the connections between individual performance, productivity, business performance, and market competitiveness.

The organization's strategic and marketing plans and objectives. To the extent you can share such information, share it! Often, managers share the organization's broad strategic initiatives with many internal and external audiences. Employees should be one of them. You should make them aware of the following:

- Where the organization is going—the Vision.
- Why the organization is going there—Strategic Intent.
- How the organization is planning to get there—Strategic Plan.
- How those in the organization will know when they get there—The BHAG.

First, share the organization's vision for the future, what it wants to be in five, ten, or fifteen years. Then explain the reasons behind that vision. These should reflect living out the organization's core purpose, such as 3M's core purpose of *providing innovative solutions to problems.*

In addition, revisit the shared values that drive the organization—the values that are the foundation of the vision.

Follow with an explanation of the strategic plan, the blueprint for getting from the present to the future. Where possible, try to tie in the role your unit has in the overall plan. Finally, share the BHAG, the Big, Hairy, Audacious Goal that—once accomplished—will signify that your organization has realized its vision.

Naturally, you can't do any of this if either your organization doesn't have a grand plan or does not wish to share it. If the former, concentrate on sharing short-term business and operational goals such as productivity or profit-margin targets. Such figures may not be exciting, but revealing them will help to keep your team focused on the job at hand.

Best Tip

Share your vision of the future with all employees. It's essential—especially if you want to have any future at all.

If senior managers don't want to share overall plans, share what you can. However, an organization that has a vision for the future and doesn't share it with employees is doomed to having no future at all.

The organization's business performance. Employees are also very interested in how the company is doing financially. Watching the company's performance is a way for them to keep score. In some cases, they are interested to see if their hard work is making a difference. Others just want to follow how the stock they bought through the employee stock-purchasing plan is performing.

The reasons don't matter. What matters is that employees are involved and concerned. Provide them with quarterly updates, at least, on business performance. Such measures as sales, productivity, profit margins, market share, and stock prices are good, easily understandable benchmarks to use. They also provide a reality check. They keep employees connected to the real world in which the business operates.

The work team's goals and objectives. Finally, ensure that every employee is familiar with the work team's goals and objectives for the year. As mentioned, your work team should have its own annual plan, a plan that's been created, in part, with input from all members of the team. The plan should define quantifiable goals and objectives, and include methods to monitor and evaluate results. Share results regularly with all employees in the work team.

Review the plan quarterly to determine how well you are doing as a group. Use the review, too, as an opportunity to fine-tune or revise the plan.

Coach

If you've ever played a sport, you know the role of a coach. The coach is part instructor, cheerleader, disciplinarian, organizer, and director. A coach brings all the parts together, much as a symphony conductor does. While the mentor focuses on developing individual potential, the coach focuses on group potential by maximizing effectiveness of individual team members and the team as a whole. In this role, your job is to:

- Enhance technical skills and competencies.
- Improve personal interaction between managers and employees, and among employees.
- Improve problem-solving skills.
- Improve employee performance.
- Increase breadth of technical understanding.
- Encourage commitment to continuous improvement and learning.

Enhance technical skills and competence. The manager must have a thorough understanding of the skills and competencies required for the team to be successful.

You need to identify employees' skill and competence levels and develop strategies for improving them.

When it is evident that an employee may not have the ability to master the skill and competencies required by a job, move that individual into a different role more suited to his or her abilities.

But don't just pass incompetence on to another manager. Rather, work to position the employee in a job either inside or outside the organization where the chance of success is high.

Improve personal interaction among team members. Enhance interaction among team members by fostering open and constant communication, and positive interpersonal skills.

By example, you set the pattern for communication. To the greatest extent possible, be available, listen rather than talk, share information openly, support rather than judge, and encourage comments and suggestions. By creating an open communication environment, you create a self-managing team.

In a *Boston Globe* story, Red Auerbach, the legendary Boston Celtics coach, was reported to have offered similar wisdom to Rick Pitino during the 1997-98 season. Auerbach suggested that when the new Celtics coach went into the huddle he should occasionally ask the players for suggestions.

Pitino relates how he did that during a crucial game and player Antoine Walker said, "How the hell do we know? You're the coach." A year later, the players were suggesting plays. Given time, experience, and encouragement, every team member can learn how to contribute and, when needed, lead.

Improve problem-solving skills. For some people, problem solving comes naturally. Others need to learn how to systematically analyze and develop a solution for a problem.

Work one-on-one with employees or arrange for training in problem-solving techniques. However you improve employee skills, employ techniques that are consistent within the team and the organization. For example, if the organization employs a Total Quality Management (TQM) approach, then TQM problem-solving techniques should be taught and used by all team members.

Improve employee performance. Performance evaluations

are very powerful tools. Unfortunately, most managers give them less than lip service. They avoid the evaluation process.

Conduct performance evaluations at least twice annually, if not more often. While a written evaluation need only be done annually, meet at least twice during the year with each employee to discuss performance and related issues.

Encourage continuous improvement in your employees. Offer them opportunities to train, learn, and gain experience in a variety of ways.

Use a written evaluation to establish performance goals for the upcoming year, and to confirm and emphasize the need for additional training and/or resources to reach the performance targets. And get input from your employees. Employees who help develop performance targets are more likely to commit themselves to achieving them.

Review goals and targets at meetings conducted periodically during the year.

Increase breadth of technical understanding. In enhancing skills and competencies, you should also strive to improve employee understanding of the technical aspects of the team's work. This may involve one-on-one coaching, group training sessions, or formal academic training.

Identify the technical knowledge to be acquired, who should acquire it, what the best training methodology is, and how to keep staff up-to-date on technological advances.

Encourage commitment to continuous improvement and learning. By emphasizing performance goal-setting, skills and competence development, and technical understanding, you instill in employees a commitment to lifelong improvement and learning.

The coach stresses a universal truth: that life is an ongoing exercise in continuous improvement through a lifetime commitment to learning.

Motivate

As a motivator, you are both a cheerleader and a disciplinarian. The motivator has to know what buttons to push on each employee.

In case you haven't noticed, individuals are unique in terms of what motivates them to action. Proof? Just look at your kids. We experience this phenomenon all the time with our children. One performs exceptionally well in school without you having to say one word. Others require a constant barrage of parental expletives just to get them to open a book, much less read it.

The trick is to find what motivates each person. Some are motivated internally, constantly energized by new challenges. Others need external motivators, like the fear of flipping burgers for the rest of their lives.

Here are some tried-and-true methods for motivating your employees (and your kids, too):

Praise. This works, even with your kids. Everybody loves praise. Not false praise but honest praise for work well-done, goals accomplished, or valued behavior displayed.

Incidentally, you can always find something to praise in an individual. As a longtime public relations practitioner, I found that I could turn the most negative, distrustful people into allies by just noticing and mentioning one thing about them that was worthy of praise. It might be how they dressed or their efficiency in producing a report. It didn't matter. The fact that I praised them sincerely was not forgotten. It also prompted them to continue that one positive behavior, a behavior that could be contagious.

Recognize and reward. Recognizing and rewarding people for positive behavior is essential. Recognition and rewards, in most cases, should be done in public forums. First, it allows the employee to bask in the spotlight before their peers. Second, employees can stand as role models for their peers as examples of behavior that is both recognized and rewarded by the organization.

Recognize employees at a department meeting, in a memorandum posted on a bulletin board, in a letter to employees, or at an annual awards banquet.

Rewarding can also occur in various forms. We all know what the research says: Money is a good reward, but only up to a point. Most people don't work hard because of the money. They want to feel good about what they do and be recognized for that work. Besides money, rewards can take the form of an award, such as a plaque or trophy, a free service, a vacation, or added responsibility and more challenging work.

Demonstrate enthusiasm. I teach in both the undergraduate and graduate level in college. My experience has taught me that unless you bring a high level of energy and enthusiasm to the classroom, you will not succeed as a teacher. People respond to those who generate enthusiasm. The more enthusiastic you are about your job, your work, and your career, the more likely it is that your employees will be enthusiastic about theirs.

Best Tip

Don't use 'one size fits all' motivational techniques. Find out what moves each individual on your team.

It's hard to ask people to be excited about the work they do when you show little excitement yourself.

Establish attainable goals. Accomplishment is a great motivator. People get energized when they accomplish a task, reach a milestone, complete a project. They can also be deflated if they fail to reach their goals. So goal-setting is important. Ensure that goals established are attainable.

Yes, by all means, set goals that are a stretch but not such a stretch that failure is likely. That's why it is important to have employee input into goal-setting.

Promote high performers. Another powerful motivational tool is promoting high performers to positions of greater responsibility.

A promotion accomplishes a number of things. First, it recognizes and rewards the high performers, motivating them to continue working at a high level.

Second, it positions your high performers in roles where they can have a greater impact on the success of your work team and/or the organization as a whole.

Third, those promoted will serve as models for others in the work team. And, lastly, promotions reinforce the culture of the organization by demonstrating that high performance is valued, recognized, and rewarded both by you and the organization.

Mentor

Unlike a coach's job, the mentor's role is not necessarily a supervisory one. The mentor can often be some other manager in the organization who is respected and trusted by the employee. Whereas the coach improves performance, the mentor enhances potential.

The mentor takes on many jobs. Mentors:

Give professional advice. The mentor serves as a professional advisor to the employer. When asked, you offer advice and counsel regarding a wide range of issues in the workplace. These issues may involve how to proceed with a job-advancement opportunity, how to deal with a personality conflict, or how to enhance work performance.

Act as confidants. Because you are trusted and respected by employees, they may seek you out for personal guidance on sensitive issues. These may involve work relationships or family issues.

Sometimes they may be very delicate emotional issues. Your primary role here is to listen. Empathize with their concerns and pain. Just by listening, you help employees work through issues.

Effective confidants employ these simple techniques:

Best Tip

Practice listening. It's a skill that serves managers especially well during times of change.

- Listen carefully to what the employee is saying. Indicate that you are listening by making eye contact.
- When the employee pauses, reiterate the last three or four words that the employee spoke. This confirms to the employee that you're listening.
- Reflect back words or phrases that express the employee's feelings, such as, "You're embarrassed by this," or "You're really upset by what was said." Such phrases help legitimize the feelings the employee is expressing.
- Avoid giving advice. Instead, ask questions that prompt the employee to begin examining alternatives for dealing with the problem. For example, "What do you think you could do to improve this situation?"

If an employee presents you with a serious personal problem, do not try to serve as a counselor. You are not a professional therapist. Refer the employee to your employee assistance program. If you don't have one, seek the assistance of your organization's human resources or employee-relations professional. That person can help identify counseling services available through the employee's health plan.

Provide performance feedback. You can provide employees an invaluable service by providing performance feedback. If you have their trust and respect, they will listen to what you have to say about job performance.

Naturally, such evaluations must be constructive. Always include suggestions for improvement where needed. Also praise, when justified, to reinforce good behaviors. In this role, you can help establish for the employee benchmarks for improving performance.

Teach political astuteness. Employees, especially those hoping to move up to a supervisory position, need to understand the political realities of organizational life. They need to appreciate and grasp the nuances of how things work in your company. Help them understand. Who, for instance, has power and who doesn't? Such knowledge will help your employee effect change without stepping on toes.

You can also tutor bright employees on how to acquire and manage power, what is and is not appropriate business and social behavior, and which skills are necessary for navigating through the maze of an organization.

Offer career counseling. Provide assistance to employees examining their options. Encourage employees to examine and plan for their futures. Provide feedback on potential career directions, and offer advice on educational and work opportunities that provide professional growth for employees. Don't so much assist in planning a career as much as encourage planning to occur.

Be a career coach. You, as mentor, also serve as a career coach. As coach, attempt to enhance employees' skills in managing their careers. This includes assisting employees in identifying strengths and weaknesses in both their technical competence and interpersonal skills; developing an appreciation for the need to manage one's career; helping them commit to their careers; helping them develop a career path; and, finally, helping employees gain a sense of control over their careers.

Begin by having the employee identify where he or she wants to be in five years and what skills, knowledge, and education they will need to get there. Then have the employee draft a plan with annual goals that leads to the desired objective five years out. If nothing more, this exercise forces people to think about the future.

Encourage risk taking. Employees often fail to live up to their potential because of fear of failure. One reason: They learn quickly that failure gets punished. So they become risk averse. They learn to play it safe.

Many organizations have a "winners and losers" mentality. The message: If you succeed, you're a winner. If you fail, you're a loser.

But many of the better organizations don't promote this unconstructive message. As mentor, you must support and encourage risk taking. Teach how to judge what are appropriate risks and what are not. Good risks are those in which the upside outweighs the downside. The question to ask is: What is the worst possible result if you fail?

As an advocate for risk taking, ensure that others in the organization understand that you support and encourage it. You will help create a more supportive and encouraging environment for the risk-taking employee.

I have an interesting story to tell here. I knew a young vice president who, at the urging of the CEO, volunteered to lead the Total Quality Management initiative being launched at our medical center.

The TQM effort would be a massive undertaking. His new job would be full-time for a two-year period. Many thought he was jeopardizing his career by leaving his secure management role to assume responsibility for what some thought to be just another management fad.

He took the project on and became a star.

The story doesn't end there. He returned to the management ranks and eventually fell victim to a major restructuring in the organization. But with his outstanding background, especially in TQM, he moved on to become CEO of a mid-sized hospital. He took a risk and in the long run it paid huge dividends for his career.

Encourage participation in high-profile activities. To promote risk taking, encourage employee participation in high profile projects or programs.

Some may be cutting edge or experimental, which could be somewhat risky for those who participate. For example, those who volunteer to participate in continuous quality improvement (CQI) efforts place themselves at risk. They are investing considerable time in process improvement that could be spent on improving their own work skills. Their CQI effort could fail to attain the desired improvement goals. The CQI initiative could fall out of favor with senior management.

All these scenarios place the employee at risk. But it is a risk worth taking because of the potential payoff: a higher profile for the employee, the ability to display various talents, the opportunity to network with management, the opportunity to make a significant contribution to the organization's success, and the acquisition of new skills and techniques.

Provide access to promotion opportunities. You have two roles here. The first is to support an employee seeking to apply for a promotion. You can both encourage the employee in seeking the position, as well as provide recommendations for the employee. The second role is to identify and position the employee for potential advancement opportunities either inside or outside the organization.

You can position employees by personally recommending them to peers and/or potential employers. You can also "talk up" employees among their peers and superiors.

The Agile Manager's Lessons Learned

✔ Be a leader. It requires decisiveness, a cool head, and the ability to understand and articulate the organization's vision and mission.

✔ Educate your employees about the changing business marketplace.

✔ Coach employees. You'll maximize the effectiveness of each one.

✔ Motivate by identifying the unique factors that enhance performance for each employee.

Chapter Three

Manage Routine Change

Wanda sat underneath the tree outside her window eating her lunch and thinking about the different changes she'd gone through.

She made a mental list of them: a minor layoff, reengineering the testing process, acquiring the modest product line of a defunct manufacturer, and the companywide switch to a self-service human resources Web site.

Pretty small stuff, she thought. Yet we accomplished each by going about the change systematically—getting our hands around the change, plugging holes in the dike if we needed to, planning action steps in detail, making sure everyone affected knew what was happening, proceeding with the plan carefully but deliberately, and then making sure the result was close enough to what we wanted.

It seems like the same process would work for a big change, too—except that there will be a lot of people I don't know making decisions about my future. Like whether I keep my job or not.

She stood up suddenly, to try to shake off the new surge of anxiety.

Recall that I defined routine change as "operational fine-tuning"—changes in policy, strategy, scheduling, introducing or abandoning products, minor process improvements, and so forth.

Using the methods outlined in this chapter will help you handle such routine changes. And it's not by accident that you'll also use these methods, in part, to handle nonroutine change. Why? Change is change. The difference lies in the extent of the change, not in its nature.

Best Tip

One way to identify the need for change: Survey the environment constantly for new developments in your industry.

So how do you manage routine change in your area of responsibility? Naturally, it all begins with identifying the need for change. Either you or your employees or your bosses identify the need for change.

You identify the need for change both by continuously reviewing the work processes in your department and continuously surveying the environment for new developments in your industry.

The process for identifying the need for change in your work area is the same that is used in Total Quality Management (TQM). In TQM, you follow these simple steps:

- Identify the processes with the most significant impact on meeting customer requirements.
- Determine which processes fail to meet or exceed customer requirements.
- Identify the processes, which if improved, will most likely have the greatest benefit to your internal or external customers.

In some cases, process failures may not be present but changes in technology, materials, equipment, or customer needs and expectations may warrant improving or totally reengineering current processes.

One of your key responsibilities is thus to stay current with developments in your field. That's how you can keep abreast— and keep your bosses abreast—of significant changes in the competitive marketplace.

In brief, here's the process for managing routine change in your workplace:

1. Identify opportunities for improvement.
2. Select the opportunity.
3. Plan and implement the change.

Develop an Implementation Plan

Once you've identified an opportunity for improvement, you must develop an implementation plan. There are six steps to developing a good plan:

1. Organize a change-implementation team.
2. Define the process to be improved and determine how much you want to improve it.
3. Implement temporary fixes, if necessary.
4. Identify problem causes.
5. Identify and implement changes that correct the problem or improve the process.
6. Evaluate the results and follow up.

Organize the team. This may be the most critical step in changing some aspect of your workplace. Get the right people on the team. Identify those with knowledge of the process or activity you want to improve.

Also, involve others from outside your work area that may be impacted by the change. They can be especially helpful in managing the change.

First, they can keep employees in their work areas informed of the plan for change. Second, they can help "sell" the change to their peers. And third, they

Best Tip

Put people from outside your department on your change team. They can help 'sell' the idea to people in their area.

can assist in working out problems the change might cause in their areas.

Other considerations for putting together your team:

—Consider placing on the team those with special technical skills or knowledge.
—Make sure you have a mix of supervisory and nonsupervisory staff.
—Include on the team anyone who has recommended the change.
—Appoint no more than twelve members.
—Appoint a team leader who has good interpersonal skills and whom all team members respect.

Define the situation. Identify, in broad terms, the change that is required. The team's responsibility is then to define the process that needs to be improved to effect the change, the size of the problem, and how success will be measured.

For example, a manager in a human resources department might see the necessity for changing how new employees are processed. The implementation team will be charged with identifying the process that has the greatest impact on processing time, how long it currently takes to process a new employee, and how much improvement is required.

Best Tip

Consider quick fixes a necessary evil. Use them if you must, but commit to solving the underlying problem.

These tasks can only be performed by those who have intimate knowledge of human resources policies and procedures, as well as those who are customers of this service.

Carry out temporary fixes. In some cases, temporary fixes are necessary to stop the bleeding. We've all had occasion to use them. You notice the kitchen sink drain is leaking. Out comes the plumber's tape. It stops the leak, but only temporarily.

That's the problem with fixes. They are stopgap measures. They usually don't last long. So when they give way, the resulting problem is often bigger than the original one. Fixes are a necessary evil. Use them only when absolutely necessary.

Identify problem causes. Successful change implementation requires not only understanding what you want to change but why you want to change it. What is causing the problem with the process? Why

> **Best Tip**
>
> To get to the root of a problem, ask yourself, "Why are we not meeting our customer's requirements and expectations?"

is it less efficient? More costly? Less productive? More labor intensive? Lower quality? Less responsive?

The change-implementation team must get at the underlying causes to what's called, in TQM, *non-conformances.* Simply put, why are we not meeting our customer's requirements and expectations? Knowing the causes prepares the team for finding solutions to improving the processes.

Identify and implement changes. With intimate knowledge of the processes, the team brainstorms potential changes. It selects those changes that have the greatest likelihood of obtaining the desired results.

Teams can evaluate proposed changes using either quantifiable or qualitative assessment tools. Quantitative tools include such things as cost/benefit or force-field analyses. Qualitative assessment may involve looking at ethical, legal, and public relations implications, or the impact on staff, customers, suppliers, and the environment.

In making such analyses, even the brightest and best among us can make errors. To avoid mistakes, the team should pre-test or proof the proposed changes.

That's what the Europeans did when they introduced the Euro, the new European currency. Prior to implementation, the sophisticated computer and software systems handling the conver-

---

Plan the Change Well

Putting change into effect requires a detailed plan. An implementation plan should comprise the following:

- Rationale for the change initiative.
- Clear and measurable objectives and goals.
- Action steps for implementing the change.
- Roles and responsibilities of those charged with implementing the plan.
- Resources required for implementation.
- Timetable for implementation.
- Evaluation measures.
- Monitoring process.

In essence, the plan lays out what is to be done. Who is to do it? What specifically has to be done step by step? What resources are required, including new equipment, facilities, training, personnel, policies, and procedures? When do we undertake each step of the action plan? How will we measure whether the plan is successful or not? How will we monitor operations following the change?

---

sion were run through their paces to work out any expected bugs. The conversion went off without a major hitch. Proofing works.

Evaluate and follow up. In defining the situation, the change-implementation team determines the extent of the changes that would have to be made to improve the process. This requires measuring the process.

In the human resources example, it would be a measure of cycle time, the time it takes to process job applicants. This measure would be used to establish a measure of success for the change effort.

The measure of success answers the question: How much do we have to reduce the cycle time for processing job applicants to significantly improve the process?

Follow up requires continuous monitoring of your process. In our example, the HR employee has been given the authority to oversee processing job applicants. As she processes each applicant, she records how long it takes her. If it takes longer than it should, she reviews each step in the process to identify where the delay is and corrects it.

This is process control. This is also the definition of employee empowerment. Employees are empowered whenever they are placed in operational control of their work processes. This creates an environment in which employees are engaged with, participating in, and supportive of change.

Communicate the Plan for Change

Once the change-implementation team has finished the plan and it is approved, share it with as many people as possible. Ensure everyone involved with or affected by the change is aware of the change and how it benefits him or her. They have to know the answer to the WAM question.

The answer, you'll often find, is that it makes work life simpler and easier for employees and managers. By making processes more efficient, change reduces hassle.

If necessary, take the plan on the road. Bring it around to every department and work area that will be affected. Involve members of the change-implementation team in the education effort. With your support, have them present the plan at their department meetings. Promote the plan in your employee newspaper or corporate magazine. Present it at management meetings. Hype it through e-mail and fax. In other words, do whatever is necessary to sell it to the masses.

Once you have made the change, monitor the process until you're sure the change improved it.

The Agile Manager's Lessons Learned

✔ First step: Identify the need for the change.

✔ Survey the business environment to identify new ideas and technologies you can use to improve operations.

✔ Review your own work processes to identify opportunities for improvement.

✔ Use teams to develop the plan for change and to gain support for the change throughout the organization.

✔ Choose well when organizing the change-implementation team.

✔ Remember: It's your responsibility to sell the change not only to your own people but also to those whose support and participation will be essential to the long-term success of the change initiative.

Chapter Four

Manage
Nonroutine Change

"And so," said the Agile Manager to the fifteen people in his department, *"it looks like it's going to happen. Top people from both companies are huddled together right now figuring out the details."*

"Our development department is better than theirs. Do the guys in the suits know that?" asked Manuel.

"I don't know," said the Agile Manager.

Anita, looking forlorn, asked, "Will we lose our jobs?"

"I don't know," said the Agile Manager.

"It seems to me they are wrecking two good companies. What's the point?" asked William.

"That's a question I can at least begin to answer," said the Agile Manager. *"As you know, two of our top competitors just joined forces. They'll have tremendous resources. Our CEO and the board figured we'd better bulk up or risk getting flattened. They—we—have a vision of becoming a global giant."*

"Yeah, but why with Murphy," said William. *"They're really stodgy."*

"They have product lines in areas we don't, but other than that I don't know," said the Agile Manager, who wondered about the

choice himself. He was beginning to see the magnitude of the task facing him. "I ran into one of the vice presidents, who promised that the intranet would have a lot of information by tomorrow afternoon, and that they'd update it regularly." I hope they do, he thought, or we might start to lose some good people.

To this point, I have discussed your role in managing routine change in your area of responsibility. But as a manager, you also have a broader role—to assist in advocating and supporting nonroutine or radical system-wide change championed by the organization's senior management. Such changes could be anything from a merger to closing a division to dropping—or adding—an entire product line.

My experience has shown me that effective communication throughout an organization is absolutely essential for implementing radical change successfully.

My last boss, a former corporate executive for a large insurance company that underwent a merger, once told me that he was amazed at the insatiable appetite employees had for information during a major change. They always had more questions than management had answers.

Before getting to the heart of this chapter—how you can use communication to manage radical change—I'd like to discuss the do's and don'ts of sharing information with employees. As you'll see, there are many pitfalls to avoid.

Big Mistake: Looking Beyond Event Horizons

For senior managers and those who counsel them, the question always is how much to say about possible future events. People are naturally inquisitive. They will ask, "Will my department close, or merge, or expand or downsize? Will I have a job? If so, will it be the same or different?"

Once you answer one question about the future you begin down a slippery slope. That slope empties into a black hole of misinformation, miscalculation, misstatements, and missteps. The result: lost credibility!

One way of addressing this issue is to think of the edge of that slippery slope as an *event horizon*. Coined by Stephen Hawking, the internationally renowned astrophysicist, the phrase refers to the outer edge of a black hole in space. A black hole is a star that has collapsed. Its mass is so dense that nothing, including light, can escape from its gravitational field. The event horizon is the point beyond which no event is observable and, therefore, knowable.

Best Tip

Don't lose your credibility by trying to predict the future. In any change effort, you need all the credibility you can get.

You know you've reached the event horizon whenever you hear a terrible sucking sound—it's you losing your credibility! And that's the worst thing that can happen to management in general and to a manager in particular. Why? Because without credibility there is no trust. And without trust you cannot lead, manage, or motivate.

Radical change creates black holes in an organization's future. It forms event horizons beyond which you cannot predict what will occur with any degree of accuracy. Management's task is to identify where in the future the event horizon lies. In other words, it must predict what is both knowable and unknowable about the future. The event horizon may be weeks, months or, perhaps, years out. Wherever it lies, management should refrain from making predictions beyond the event horizon.

This lesson was painfully driven home for me when I served as an executive for a large medical center. We had just completed a merger with two other hospitals. In meetings with employees at all three hospitals, the new CEO proudly announced that, rather than layoffs, the merger would create more jobs and opportunities for professional growth. He believed it. We all believed it.

Six months later, we closed one of the hospitals, laying off 250 employees. We had stepped beyond the event horizon. We made a promise about an unknowable future. We destroyed our credibility. It was a loss that would haunt us for years to come.

| **Best** **Tip**

Remember: It's OK to say 'I don't know,' or, 'That's impossible to predict.' These are credible responses.

We paid a high price for learning that you can never be sure about the long-term effects of radical change. To try to predict or guarantee events lying beyond the event horizon is folly. We also learned an invaluable lesson: When asked about the future it's OK to say, *"I don't know,"* or *"That's impossible to predict."* These are human, credible responses. You are hereby given permission to use them.

To Share, or Not to Share

Truth is, the more radical the change, the lower the accuracy in predicting future events. That's a function of the long time line and the large number of uncontrollable variables associated with such change. Radical change tends to be both complex and highly dynamic.

Consequently, when you know the answers to specific questions, you may not or cannot share them because of their sensitive, strategic nature.

For example, you may enter into a merger to gain some market advantage. This may be information you want to share with your employees. However, you have to be careful not to reveal too much. You may, for example, choose to speak in general terms about positioning in the marketplace without necessarily revealing the specifics of strategic and tactical initiatives.

But it is precisely this kind of specific information that will be sought by your staff because they have a vested interest in the merger.

While there are strategic reasons for not sharing information, there are practical reasons as well. If given more information than requested or needed, people become overwhelmed. They can, and often do, suffer information overload. They don't know what to do with the information, and they don't know how to respond to it.

With your workforce already feeling at risk, the lack of information about the future can further heighten anxiety and fear. Such feelings can lead, naturally, to increased resistance to the change and anger towards those responsible for advocating the change. And you can make the situation even worse if you are either unduly callous or ineffectual in your communication efforts.

By now it should be obvious that your role as a communicator is central to mastering change. You need to know what to say, how to say it, and when to say it. The art of effective communication, in fact, may be the agile manager's most important skill.

Tap the Power of Strategic Communication

An essential component for implementing nonroutine change is strategic communication. Let's begin by first discussing how senior management can use communication strategically to further its aims. Then we'll talk about how you can both support senior management's initiatives and manage nonroutine change in your work area.

Simply stated, the role of strategic communication is to further the strategic objectives of the organization. You do that by developing mutual understanding between the organization and its key constituencies in a way that earns their trust, cooperation, and support. Constituencies, also known as stakeholders,

|Best Tip

Plan to know what to say, how to say it, and when to say it. Artful communication may be your most important skill.

include employees, vendors, customers, shareholders, and community members.

This is the science. The art lies in knowing when, where, how, and why. It also involves knowing how much information to share.

As noted earlier, it is just as dangerous to provide too much information as too little. The rule to follow here is a simple one. Good parents apply it all the time when teaching their children about sensitive issues, such as the big S word—SEX! When a child asks a question, such as "How does the baby get in mommy's tummy?", simply tell the child to ask your spouse. Works for me.

Seriously, do what the good parent does: Answer the question being asked. No more, no less. If you provide more information than is needed or asked, the child becomes confused or conflicted. The same is true for adults.

Naturally, the information needed will differ for each constituency. The extent and the timing of information provided will be directly related to the interests of the particular constituency. Responding to these varying information needs requires a well-planned, comprehensive, strategic communication effort.

Communication goals for each constituency will differ during any change initiative. For example, your goals in communicating with employees could be to:

- Reduce organizational anxiety.
- Engender support for the change initiative.
- Enable employees to deal with ambiguity.

Use Integrated Strategic Communication

The most effective approach to implementing a comprehensive communication strategy is to integrate all organizational communication. This means centrally controlling message strategy, content, and delivery. This is Integrated Strategic Communication (ISC).

It is senior management's job to manage this process. Organizationally, responsibility for implementing strategic communication initiatives is assigned to the company's formal communications function, usually the public relations department.

In a study of business process reengineering at insurer CIGNA, researchers listed communicating "truthfully, broadly and via multiple forums" as one of the ten lessons learned for successfully implementing radical change in an organization. "It is important for those who will be affected by reengineering to understand how the effort will unfold and how it will affect them as individuals," wrote the researchers.

The CIGNA experience reflects the philosophy employed in Integrated Strategic Communication. The ISC philosophy is similar to the approach advocated by gurus and practitioners of integrated marketing communications, an approach consistent with what we know works in successfully mastering change. ISC is based on the following model:

When people ask questions about a change, answer the question being asked—no more, no less.

1. Identify your target audiences and learn as much as you can about them.

2. Identify what target audience behaviors you want to influence.

3. Identify what it is that we need to say to target audiences to influence behavior.

4. Determine how you want to say it.

5. Identify when and where the best time to say it is.

6. Select the best means possible for transmitting the message.

7. Deliver the message frequently and consistently.

8. Change the message as necessary.

9. Monitor, evaluate, and follow-up what you've said, how you've said it, and whom you've said it to.

This basic model guides the ISC approach to promoting understanding and support for major organizational change.

How to Use ISC to Implement Change

To successfully implement change, you need to gain the support of each key constituency. To gain that support, you must figure out the answer to the WAM question (What about me?) for each group. Once you know the answer, you can develop an appropriate communication strategy for each.

To gain the support of each constituency in the organization, be able to answer the question, 'What about me?' for each group.

One key aspect of your communication strategy is to come up with an overarching theme for the change initiative. The theme should be a brief, compelling argument that explains the primary benefit of the change for the target audience members.

When Hologic, Inc., merged in 1996 with Fluoroscan Imaging, Inc., the Hologic president sold the merger as the "first step in Hologic's strategy to diversify into markets that we believe offer accelerated growth potential in the upcoming years. Furthermore, we expect that the utilization of Hologic's extensive international distribution network will greatly assist Fluoroscan in its efforts to penetrate overseas markets where it has previously had minimal presence."

The simple, underlying message: increased market share and profits ensure long-term growth and financial stability. These are succinct, persuasive reasons for Hologic and Fluoroscan employees, management, and shareholders to throw their support behind the merger.

Your Role in Strategic Communication

While most managers don't control the strategic communication process, they do play an important and indispensable role. They are a key and often critical means of communicating with employees. As a matter of fact, researchers in organizational communication have found that employees consider their immediate supervisors the most reliable and credible source of information.

In a strategic communication role, managers are responsible for the following:

- Implementing message strategies.
- Reinforcing message strategies.
- Monitoring the effect of message strategies.
- Ensuring employees have access to organizational media.

Implementing message strategies. Once a communication strategy is developed, senior management must create separate message strategies for each target audience. When Bell Atlantic and NYNEX announced their 1996 merger, the new vice chairman expressly addressed employee concerns of job security. In the merger announcement, he said, "We will continue to act responsibly toward our employees, especially those affected by this merger, and will continue to aggressively pursue redeployment opportunities for affected personnel."

He also noted that when Bell Atlantic NYNEX Mobile was created, the company initially experienced job reductions followed by "significant marketplace expansion, redeployment, and the creation of new jobs."

Your role is to ensure that such information is shared with your

Best Tip

Ponder well: Studies show that employees consider their immediate supervisors the most credible source of information.

employees. You are also responsible for ensuring that the information is accurate, that every member of the work team has access to the information, and that the information is delivered on a timely basis. You don't want your employees receiving information that has already been shared with other employees the day before or, worse, that they've read in the morning's newspaper.

Reinforcing message strategies. In your role as educator, you reinforce message strategies by enhancing employee understanding of the marketplace. By keeping employees informed of what is happening in your industry and among your competitors, you help put current organizational strategies in perspective. Employees are more likely to buy into a merger strategy, such as Hologic's, if they perceive the organization's actions as consistent with the reality of the marketplace.

> **Best Tip**
>
> Let senior managers know how their messages are being received in the field. Assist them in fine-tuning messages.

Monitoring the effect of message strategies. You are also responsible for assisting senior managers in fine-tuning message strategies. Your job is to provide both your own assessment of the message strategies, as well as any feedback you get from employees.

As you discuss major change initiatives with your employees, take note of their issues, problems, and concerns. Relay these to senior management, indicating how you responded and requesting additional information or clarification if necessary. When forwarding employee comments, be precise and explicit. Don't hold anything back. Take notes and record employee comments and questions as accurately as possible.

And remember: If you don't know the answer to a question, don't fabricate one. Just say, "I don't know, but I'll try to get a response for you."

Senior management has to know how the message is being received in the field. Only then can it review and candidly assess its communication strategy. This information can also be shared with other managers, ensuring that communications are consistent throughout the organization.

Ensuring access to organizational media. Managers are

also responsible for ensuring that their employees have access to the organization's formal communication media. These include Intranet bulletin boards, e-mail, newsletters, auto-attended voice message systems, bulletin board postings, closed-circuit television programs, unit and department meetings, companywide employee meetings, shareholder reports, annual reports, and mailings.

If you hold meetings for your employees, ensure everyone has the opportunity to attend. If necessary, schedule additional meetings to cover all shifts.

In addition to supporting the implementation of nonroutine or radical change throughout the organization you may also have to manage how those changes affect your work area. So let's discuss that next.

Manage Nonroutine Change Locally

Nonroutine change is always far more disruptive and affects far more people than does routine change. It also requires an information-rich environment for success. Hence, managing nonroutine change is, more often than not, very difficult and challenging. You will need all of your skills as a changemaster to successfully manage nonroutine change.

In my many years in management, I've been involved in implementing numerous radical changes in various organizations. While there is no formula or precise model for managing radical change, I have been able to identify a number of strategies that have worked for me. Let me share them with you:

1. Focus employees on the organization's vision.

2. Reinforce the case for change as it reflects the vision.

3. Identify how the change will affect your work area and employees.

4. Provide employees with a plan for managing the effects of change.

5. Keep employees focused on their jobs.

6. Create a support system of employees who are committed to the change initiative.

Let's briefly discuss each of these strategies.

Focus employees on the organization's vision. Radical change is almost always implemented as a strategy for living out your vision. It's much easier for employees to understand such change when it is understood in the context of a vision. Continuously remind employees of where it is the organization is going and how it plans to get there. With a shared vision comes a shared commitment to see that vision realized.

Reinforce the case for change as it reflects the vision. As discussed, one of your primary roles is to reinforce with your employees the case for change made by senior management. The case for change is always strengthened when change is communicated as part of a strategy to realize the vision, whether that vision is to be the number one manufacturer of computer chips in the world or an auto dealership with the highest customer service rating in the industry.

Best Tip
To ensure people don't get too distracted or upset over a change, keep them focused on the job or task at hand.

Identify how the change will affect your work area and employees. As a manager, you need to anticipate how a proposed radical change will affect your area and your employees. Will you be merged, downsized, transferred? Will your roles and responsibilities change? Will staff be affected? Will management change?

By doing your homework you can begin to plan how you're going to deal with potential changes that may be required of both you and your employees. You'll also be better prepared to start to think about how you're going to respond to questions from employees about the future.

Provide employees with a plan for managing the effects of change. Having done your homework, you can now plan for how to deal with the effects of radical change on your work area. The same planning techniques discussed in chapter three for managing routine change can be applied here. The planning process for implementing change is the same whether it's routine or radical. What may be different is the amount of resources required to implement the change.

Keep employees focused on their jobs. I can't emphasize this enough. With radical change, people often become distracted and anxious. They can become so concerned with the change effort and/or the effects of the change on them and their co-workers that they fail to do their jobs. By keeping employees focused on their day-to-day tasks you help employees concentrate their energies on activities that they are both comfortable with and competent at. This lessens anxiety by giving employees a sense of control over their work environment.

Create a support system of employees who are committed to the change initiative. To successfully manage change, you will need both the support and participation of your employees. Here's a successful strategy for doing so.

First, identify those employees who are committed to change and who understand that it is essential for the success of the organization. Next, enlist their help in engendering the support of their peers in the change effort. Use them as conduits for keeping employees informed.

Your employee network of changemasters can be among your most effective tools for instilling in your workforce a commitment to change.

So now you have a game plan for managing both routine and nonroutine change in your work area. But don't think you know it all just yet. Change is a very complex phenomena. It is best managed when it is well understood. In the next few chapters we'll discuss understanding and managing loss in the workplace, why people resist change and how to overcome that resistance, and, finally, how to deal with the stress that comes with change.

The Agile Manager's Lessons Learned

✔ To manage radical change successfully, employ communications strategically.

✔ Don't try to predict the future beyond the "event horizon." You put your credibility at risk otherwise.

✔ When the future is unknown, qualify your answers to specific questions.

✔ Develop mutual understanding with key groups through strategic communication.

✔ When implementing a change, know whom to communicate with, what to say to them, how to say it, when to say it, and where to say it.

✔ Gain the support of any group by being able to answer the question, "What about me?"

✔ To help employees adapt to radical change, keep them focused on the vision—where the organization is going and how it plans to get there.

Chapter Five

Understand Change And Loss in the Workplace

It was a week after the news of the merger hit. There was a new rumor afloat—that the organization and all its people would be subordinate to Murphy Technology. The intranet page devoted to news of the merger didn't mention anything of the sort, but several people said they had it "on good authority."

"What am I supposed to do if I find myself working for a jerk," asked William angrily. "It's hard enough doing my job without having to prove myself all over again."

"Yeah," said Manuel. "And what if we have to move? They have plants all over the place—and none of them are in places that I would want to live."

"Look," said Wanda. "We don't know what's going to happen, so don't waste your time speculating. Besides, I'm convinced that nothing bad is going to happen to us. We're all too valuable. Look at how many awards we've received." She smiled serenely, having discovered a few days ago that not thinking about the merger made her feel much, much better.

She looked over at Phil, who seemed to be wiping tears from his eyes. She did a double-take. Could Phil, an engineer's engineer, actually be crying?

"Everything OK there, Phil?" she asked quietly. When he realized people were looking at him, he put his glasses back on and walked out.

While we don't like to admit it, one major reason why change is difficult is because it involves loss.

Think about it. Any time there is a change, whether in your personal life or in your work life, it involves some form of loss. It could be the loss of old responsibilities, or the comfort zone you once had because you knew everyone and they knew you. Now it's changed. What use to be is gone, forever.

That kind of loss can manifest itself as simple anxiety or, in some cases, extreme depression. It's no wonder that many individuals suffer a variety of ailments, some life threatening, when confronted with workplace loss.

According to psychologists, there are two kinds of loss that we experience in the workplace.

The first occurs whenever we change the workplace to any extent. Whenever it becomes different in any significant way, we experience a feeling of loss. The second involves the personal changes that occur. More precisely, it boils down to the WAM question: "How does the change affect me?"

Loss of a Familiar Workplace

Loss associated with a familiar workplace can occur either because of separation from a workplace for a short or long period, or because a person relocates permanently from one job site to another.

There are many reasons for such separation. It can occur because people are reassigned for temporary duty to another plant, are missing from their job for a long period because of an illness or domestic crisis, are permanently reassigned; or because they lose their jobs.

Job loss. Naturally, the most devastating kind of loss of a familiar workplace is when people lose their jobs. Not only do employees grieve over the loss of the job and its effects on their self-esteem, but they must also deal with the loss of their friends and co-workers.

For most of us, jobs help define who and what we are. And those we work with and work for help to shape how we view ourselves. Once that context is lost, employees can feel abandoned and adrift. They find it difficult to redefine themselves and to establish new meaning for their lives. Loss of a job can be among the most traumatic events.

Change in job assignment. Not nearly as devastating as losing a job, a job reassignment can still cause feelings of separation and loss. Often, job reassignments reflect management's confidence in an employee and, therefore, can be seen as a positive action. But even so, when an employee leaves familiar territory for less familiar turf, there is always a sense of loss about what has been left behind.

$Best$ Tip
With a significant change in the workplace or in work roles, expect employees to feel a significant sense of loss.

Initially, in being relocated, employees must reestablish the routine of their work lives. In addition to the routine, they must go about the arduous task of reestablishing relationships with new co-workers and relearning the culture of the new workplace.

Meanwhile, the support and positive input and strokes they received from co-workers, friends, and supervisors are no longer readily available. They have to make it on their own. This state of uncertainty can create high levels of anxiety that can seriously affect job performance, as well as the emotional health of each individual.

I've had many jobs in my life. I've worked in a variety of organizations, mostly large ones. Whenever I went to a new job I always had to deal with the anxious knot-in-the-pit-of-your-stomach feeling. The feeling that tells you that you are entering unknown territory, and so beware. While I liked the challenge of a new job, the strange environment always threw me off. It altered my routine.

A routine helps give rhythm to your day. You know exactly what to expect. The level of uncertainty is therefore lower, as is the anxiety. When routine is disturbed by a change in location, the sense of security we normally feel in the workplace disappears. It's replaced by insecurity. These feelings are, of course, worsened because we no longer have friends and co-workers to turn to for emotional support—no one to talk to, no one who understands.

Loss of co-workers. I touched on this topic earlier, but it's worth repeating. Co-workers are an important part of the workplace. They help define who we are. They are also emotional supports for us in the stormy seas of organizational life. We count on them being there when we need them.

Not too long ago, the mother of a co-worker of mine died. I visited during the calling hours. A good number of the people attending were from our company. Co-workers become, for most of us, part of our lives.

Best Tip

Understand that co-workers help define who we are at work. If we lose them, we lose part of ourselves.

In fact, losing co-workers may even be more anxiety provoking than a change in the workplace. They are like actors in a play that's called *Your Life*. Imagine going on stage and finding all the actors who are supposed to be there feeding you your lines, interacting with you, and creating the scenes for you, are gone. It's just you on an empty stage.

That's how you can feel when you lose co-workers—alone and at a loss for knowing what you should do and how you should act.

Some people experience the loss of co-workers with the same intensity they suffer when losing a significant other. That's how deeply such a loss can be felt. That is also why many of us maintain relationships with co-workers many years after leaving a company.

Loss of a Part of Self

This kind of loss includes the loss of self-esteem, self-confidence, respect, power, or love. Wait a minute—love? Yes, love. It is surprising to find that, for some people, the workplace is the only place in their lives where they feel true love and affection.

Incidentally, love can be a powerful emotion for compelling people to action. When a manager is truly loved by his staff, it will do anything in its power to ensure that he or she is successful. While rare, there are those bosses who are truly loved by the people who work for them.

Best Tip

Ponder well: You and your organization have the power to raise or lower the self-esteem of most employees.

Now don't get the idea that I'm advocating that you work to become loved by your staff. No, that's not the point. The point is that love can and does exist in the workplace. When it is lost, there is grief. And that's something you need to be aware of.

Self-esteem. Actions taken by an organization can lower self-esteem by lowering the perceived status or position of the individual. So when a company discharges or demotes an employee, takes away duties and responsibilities, reassigns him or her to a less important job, or cuts pay, it can lead to a loss of self-esteem.

I had to discharge an employee once because of severe cutbacks to save money. She was competent, pleasant, and worked well with everyone. When I told her that we were letting her go, she was emotionally devastated. She couldn't understand why she was chosen.

I met with her on a number of occasions to reinforce the fact, which was true, that letting her go had nothing to do with her job performance. I worked to bolster her ego and her sense of self-worth. I also supported her job search by making telephone calls and writing letters of recommendation. The fact that I believed she was worth helping served to reinforce her self-image. She eventually found a job and today, many years later, we remain friends.

Self-confidence. As seen in this anecdote, the loss of self-esteem is closely associated with a loss of self-confidence. When your self-image has been severely damaged, it's difficult, if not impossible, to find the confidence to be successful.

Losing a job, responsibilities, and authority are not pleasant events to live through. When people experience them, they feel they are being punished and, in many cases, they are. So naturally, there is the sense that they've done something wrong. In some way they have failed to measure up. This failure corrodes self-esteem and destroys self-confidence.

If you keep an employee you've demoted or whose responsibilities you've diminished, do your best to give the person meaningful work that he or she can feel good about doing and can succeed at.

Power. Whenever you reduce the responsibilities and/or authority of employees, you reduce their power. Doing so is always fraught with danger. That's because personal power is associated with our feelings of both security and control. To the extent that we have power we have both. Remove it and you place people at risk. They feel threatened, insecure, and impotent.

We've all heard the anecdotal stories about the senior executive who is told first thing in the morning that he's fired. He is immediately escorted to his office where, under the watchful gaze of a security guard, he cleans out his desk. Then, he's walked to his car and he drives off into the sun or off a cliff.

Does this ever happen? You bet it does, and more often than we'd like to think. Why? The loss of power, that's why! It can drive an individual to wreak revenge or strike out against the employer. Some get revenge by stealing clients, others by sabotaging computer systems, others by selling industrial secrets, and still others by stealing intellectual property. Power is as difficult to give up as it is to acquire.

Respect. Respect is related to both power and self-esteem. It is our perception of the deference people pay to us because of who we believe ourselves to be. Like Don Corleone, Mario Puzo's Godfather, that's all we really want: respect. And like the capo di tutti capi, the Mafiosi respected Don Corleone for both who he was and the power he wielded.

When you reduce an individual's power and self-esteem, you alter the respect with which he is held. In some cases, no respect may be lost, but the individual's perception may be that he has lost face and therefore respect. So when implementing change that affects individuals, treat them with respect and kindness. Be a role model in this regard for others, who will follow your lead. For most of us, respect is as important as it was to the Godfather.

Recognize that employees who have experienced a loss must work through a five-stage grieving process.

Understand the Grieving Process

When we suffer any significant loss, we have to adapt to that loss. We do that through the grieving process.

We grieve whether we've lost friends and co-workers or our self-esteem. It's healthy. It is the way that we adjust and move on from the loss.

It's important for agile managers to understand the grieving process and how it manifests itself in employee behavior. By understanding the psychological aspects of grief you'll be better able to assist your employees in adapting to loss and in managing change associated with that loss.

While each individual responds to loss differently, we know the stages of grief are universal. Elisabeth Kübler-Ross developed a behavioral model for understanding grief that is very helpful. Most of us are familiar with Kübler-Ross because of her seminal work on death and dying. Even if you've never heard of her, you'll recognize the stages in her model from your own experience dealing with employees.

The model has five stages: denial, anger, bargaining, depression, and acceptance. It all sounds familiar now, doesn't it?

Best Tip

Expect employees to bargain to prevent the loss from happening. It's a stage they need to pass through.

Denial. In the initial stage, the employee acts as though nothing has happened or refuses to believe that a change is occurring or that they are affected by it. "Hey, you can't mean me. I've been the best worker on the line!" "They can't really mean they're moving the entire division to the West Coast!"

Denial can be brief or long-term. Watch for these kinds of behaviors: Employee aggressively denies the reality of the situation; refuses to listen to those trying to help him; rejects offers of assistance or help; and fails to use services offered to him, such as talking to a counselor or outplacement personnel.

Anger. Next, the employee fights back, resisting the loss by acting out his or her fears and frustrations. "Damn them! I'm going to make them pay for what they've done to me." "These people never think about anyone but themselves. They don't care who they hurt."

More often than not the anger is internalized or not acted on. However, the more serious the loss, the greater the danger that the employee may act out his anger. Be careful in these situations.

Many years ago, when I worked at General Electric, they made a decision to sell a major product line. They had to lay off a number of employees. They told them late Friday afternoon so they could get them out of the plant as soon as possible.

I thought the timing rather callous, but more seasoned veterans told me it was the smart thing to do. If you tell them earlier, they explained, they'd act on their anger by damaging and/or stealing equipment. It had happened often in the past.

Whether right or wrong, the fact is that employees do feel anger when they suffer a loss. And sometimes that anger can be destructive to themselves and their employer.

The agile manager should watch for these telltale anger-driven behaviors: Employee retaliates and/or threatens retaliation against managers, supervisors, co-workers, friends and family members; feels guilt from acting out toward those the employee depends on; experiences increased anxiety and a lowering of self-esteem.

Bargaining. Having passed through those initial stages of denial and anger, the employee now begins to bargain. This is a familiar psychological exercise that we've all gone through. We all can remember sitting at our school desks in quiet prayer, "God, help me pass this exam and I won't forget to do my chores for a month."

We bargain all the time. In bargaining, we attempt to postpone the inevitable. We try to prevent the loss from occurring. "What if I agree to take a pay cut?" "I'll take the transfer if you can give me a few more months here."

You'll begin to see signs of fear at this stage: The employee acknowledges as real and inevitable the loss of a job, title, responsibilities, or promotion; uses or takes advantage of any opportunity to avoid the loss; and becomes open to suggestions or alternatives to help deal with the loss.

Depression. Confronted with the reality that all the bargaining in the world will not change the situation, people become depressed. They isolate themselves from everyone, even those they love.

The agile manager must be sensitive to personality changes in employees in this stage. While common, depression can be long lasting and dangerous to the health and well being of the sufferer.

Behaviors to look for: employee withdraws from close relationships with family, friends, and/or co-workers; is unusually introverted and non-communicative; lacks concern for personal hygiene and appearance; and exhibits self-destructive behaviors.

Acceptance. Having transited all these stages, hopefully intact, employees now accept the loss. They begin to return to being themselves and to resuming their relationships.

These behaviors are apparent in this stage: the employee accepts the loss; begins planning for the future; looks at alternative courses of action; and talks openly about feelings, fears, anxieties, hopes, and aspirations.

Naturally, people pass through these stages differently.

Also, the length of each stage differs. While many pass through these stages quickly, others may become stuck in anger or depression or some other stage. This is called dysfunctional grief.

It is important to understand that we all grieve to some extent for losses that occur in the workplace. Grieving is natural, beneficial, and essential. By recognizing why we grieve and how we grieve, you can better assist the employee in managing loss and adapting to change.

Indeed, this is one of your primary jobs as a leader.

Poignant moments in our nation's history reflect our need to grieve. The death of President Kennedy was one. Another: the Challenger disaster, in which Christa McAullife died. The death of the New Hampshire schoolteacher was especially disturbing to school-age children. It was President Reagan who helped our nation's children, as well as we adults, to move through our grief with what I believe to be his finest speech. In that radio address he gave us all permission to grieve for our loss and to be inspired by the courage of the astronauts.

Now that you understand the nature of loss in the workplace, we'll move on to managing that loss.

The Agile Manager's Lessons Learned

✔ Understand how people cope with loss. It'll help you manage change better.

✔ Realize that, for every change implemented in the workplace, some loss occurs.

✔ Be aware that the most personally devastating kind of loss is the loss of a job.

✔ Be sensitive. Employees can experience a loss of self-esteem when their jobs change.

✔ Help employees handle grief by first understanding that, without grief, they can never resolve their sense of loss.

✔ Help employees come to terms with a loss, and they'll adapt to change better.

Chapter Six

Manage the Sense Of Loss in the Workplace

". . . so there it is. I'll be in charge of product development, and Murphy's current head will be my number two. I'm sorry, Wanda. I fought hard for you." The Agile Manager briefly held her hand.

"I'm . . . out of a job, right?" she said, biting her lip.

"Oh no!" said the Agile Manager, relieved to be able to give her some good news. "You'll go back to managing your own projects, just like before."

She remained silent for a moment, then said, "But I won't have anyone under me, I'll get my salary reduced, and I'll lose any chance of moving into your job some day." She spoke in a monotone, looking off into the distance.

"Wanda," he said, "I'll create some opportunities for you. I promise. And don't forget—you were a great developer."

"Thanks," she said with a hint of venom in her voice. "A lot of good it did me."

"You have a perfect right to be angry," said the Agile Manager, encouraging her to vent a little more.

"After all the hours I spent helping build this department," she suddenly said, "all the weekends, all the nights, all the road trips I didn't want to go on . . ."

The Agile Manager braced himself but thought, keep going Wanda, let it all out.

After reading the last chapter, you're probably asking yourself, "What am I suppose to be, a shrink?" No, not quite. But the reality for all managers is that you do have to deal with the behavior of your employees. And that behavior is significantly affected by change.

As we saw in the previous chapter, one important effect of change is the sense that something, often something very valuable, is lost: either a job, a position, a title, responsibilities, authority, respect, co-workers, friends, or a familiar workplace. Such a loss can have a serious effect on the work performance of employees and their ability to adapt to change.

Your job is to ensure that employees move through periods of change, accept and adapt to losses, and continue to function at a high level. That is part and parcel of managing change in your organization.

In this chapter I'm going to discuss how you can help employees manage their losses in the workplace. I'll discuss the following:

- Using open communication to facilitate the grieving process.
- Assisting employees in coming to terms with their loss.
- Helping employees get back on track at work.

My aim isn't to turn you into a professional counselor. Rather, it is to help you sharpen your communication skills so you can help employees accept and adapt to loss and change in the workplace.

Promote Open Communication

One of your major responsibilities as a manager is to communicate effectively and frequently with your staff. The proper use of communication skills can have a significant impact on the success of the change efforts your organization initiates. These skills, however, aren't much good unless you promote an atmosphere of open communication.

What does that mean? By open I simply mean that the communication process is two-way. You have to learn to listen as well as to speak. Moreover, you have to create an environment in which employees feel free to talk openly with you about subjects that may be both emotionally charged and personally sensitive.

In one organization I worked in, rumors were running rampant about a potential merger. One department director was especially anxious. Whenever he saw me, he felt comfortable stopping to talk, mostly about his job. I'd spend as much time as he wanted helping him deal with his anxieties.

My message to him was a simple one: Don't worry about what the organization is going to do. You can't control that. Instead, take control of the situation by focusing on what you are going to do to position yourself for success either inside or outside of the organization.

Those little talks helped. He's still there, doing quite well—and I'm gone!

"Just as any relationship requires honest and open communication to stay healthy," notes Max DePree, "so the relationships within corporations improve when information is shared accurately and freely."

There are many ways to communicate with people. Often, we are interested only in trying to tell our sides of things. We want people to hear what we have to say, think the way we want them to think, and persuade them to do what we want them to do. We give them the impression that we want to hear what they have to say.

We may even seem to listen to them, nodding our heads in agreement—all the time waiting for that moment we can jump in and tell them exactly what we want them to hear. We are not interested in what they have to say as we are in getting them to do what we want them to do. In other words, communication is two-sided, but only so you can deliver your message.

Ultimately, this approach doesn't work. People know when they are being preached to. They know when you're not listening, really listening, to what they have to say. And they know when you're not interested in them or their problems.

I recall one day leaving my office building when a co-worker I knew drove up to me. I said hello and she began to cry. She was very upset—and this was a manager who did not get rattled easily.

I was concerned. She had just taken a new position in the organization with a new boss, another woman who had a rather bad reputation as a manager, and was having great difficulty dealing with her.

I talked to her for about fifteen minutes, sharing some thoughts with her. She thanked me. About a week later she ran

Best Tip

Show genuine concern for employees and their issues and problems as you all move through a change.

into me in the cafeteria. She told me that she had followed my advice and things were better. She thanked me both for the advice and—more important—for taking the time to listen.

To be an effective communicator, you must show genuine interest and concern for employees and their issues and problems. The communication process must be centered on working those issues out for mutual benefit. Such an approach works for both individuals and groups.

Communicate effectively one-on-one. The first step is to be open.

You've all heard about the CEO "open door" policy. The door is open all right, but no one dares walk in. What managers need is not an "open door" but rather an "open time" policy. Establish a feeling among your employees that you are always willing to spend the time and effort to talk, anywhere, anytime. "Open" means exactly that. You are open to employees and their issues, concerns, fears, and hopes.

So you're open. What now?

Part of being open is being concerned, showing empathy for employees and their problems. How do you empathize? By listening carefully and demonstrating that you are listening. Repeat key phrases or words that they've used. Nod to show that you hear what they are saying and that you acknowledge their fears, concerns, anxieties, and anger.

What they are looking for from you isn't necessarily resolution or a solution to their problem. What they are looking for is validation. Your communication task is to validate their feelings. To say, without saying it, that they have a right to feel the way they do.

By the way, sometimes these sessions can be very emotional for an employee. Stay with him throughout your meeting. Don't leave, especially if he is emotionally distraught. Make sure no one interrupts, regardless of who it might be. You want the employee to know that, while you're together, your focus is entirely on him.

Sometimes just being with people, showing empathy for their situations, helps them cope. Also, by remaining with them, you send a message that regardless of the situation, they can rely on your support.

Allow employees to 'vent' by asking open-ended questions like, 'So how does all this make you feel?'

When talking to the employee, use open-ended questions like "So how did that feel?" or "What do you think about that?" You want to keep the discussion going so the employee has a chance to work out the issue. When given the chance to talk, people can not only identify the problem confronting them but also workable solutions to those problems. The trick is to get them to think about and talk about the issue.

I recall counseling one employee who was having work difficulties with another staff member. This other person, she claimed, wasn't pulling her weight in the department. She wanted to know how to handle it. I simply asked her, "What do you think we should do?" She came up with a number of alternative approaches, some of which were very good and worked quite well. Sometimes that's all employees really need—a good sounding board for their own ideas. You, the agile manager, can be that sounding board.

Finally, allow employees to verbalize their fears. Don't try to rationalize or convince them that their fears are groundless. If someone fears losing their job or being demoted, the fear is real even if the event isn't. What you must deal with is the fear. Allow the employee to talk about these fears. Put them out front, recognize them for what they are: the result of anxiety caused by the environment of change we all live in.

That doesn't mean the employee won't lose his job or be demoted. What it means is that you acknowledge the fear associated with these possible events and, once recognized, you and the employee can rationally address those fears.

Communicate effectively with groups. Communicating with groups offers a much different challenge than communicating with an individual employee. For one thing, the anxiety level may be higher because you're before a group. Some do well before groups, many do not. You need to work at developing speaking skills if you're going to be addressing large groups.

Moreover, preparation may be more intense, because questions may be wide ranging. Nevertheless, some of the approaches discussed above can also be applied to group communication.

For example, when addressing groups, acknowledge their concerns as a group. While each employee will ultimately be concerned with the WAM question (What About Me?), concerns will be couched frequently in terms of the group. For instance, instead of the question "What about my job?," you'll hear, "Are we going to lose anyone from our department?"

The questions can also be much more dangerous. Remember that event horizon. Don't get sucked in. Be well prepared for all those hypothetical questions. "What if this happens . . ." or "What if we merge . . ." Use the standard reply: "It's impossible for me to tell you what's going to happen in the future. I don't know. The boss doesn't know. But what I do know is what I'm sharing with you now."

Show empathy with the group. Demonstrate that you understand their issues and concerns. Answer as many questions as you can. And for questions that you believe you can get an answer to, jot the question down and promise to get back to the employee who asked it and to the group as a whole with the answer. Then be sure to get back to them with a response.

Also, if you have a question in one group that no one in any other group has asked yet and may be of interest to it, share the question and answer with the group.

Be candid and have a sense of humor. It helps not only to break the tension but also to demonstrate that you're a person just like them with the same concerns and issues. Humor also tends to give another perspective on an issue—one that can be both disarming and insightful.

I remember my former CEO being put on the spot during one of our employee meetings. An employee asked why the CEO had a special parking spot next to the main building while everyone else had to suffer with the parking garage. "I get the parking space because I'm the president!" he said smiling. You had to laugh at that line and everyone did. Rank, after all, does have its privileges.

Group meetings are also a good venue for what I like to call the stump speech. It's where you energize the troops for the challenge of adapting to change ahead. Don't forget your role as cheerleader. This is the perfect opportunity to play that role. It's the moment to share a vision of your collective future, and to underscore each employee's important role in making the vision a reality.

It is also a unique opportunity to deliver the message that change isn't all that bad. As I've noted, it's what keeps us motivated, alive, and vital. As my former CEO would often say to our gathered throng of managers: "Had enough change lately?" "No!" replied the throng, "Not yet!" They still haven't!

Assist Employees in Resolving Loss

Let's go back to Kübler-Ross's framework for understanding the stages of loss. In each stage, managers have a role to play. Let's look at each in turn.

Resolving Denial. Begin by being empathetic. Demonstrate a caring manner. Use a soft tone of voice and try to maintain a position relatively close to the employee. Explain that denial, anger, and all the other responses that the employee will be experiencing are natural and expected. Don't rush the employee in the belief that they should "get over" their denying what has happened. Give them time. They'll eventually come around.

Working through Anger. Remember, anger is expected. Accept it and be tolerant of it. Show that you understand the employee's anger. And, what ever you do, don't take it personally. Much of this anger may be directed at you because you delivered the bad news.

You may also find some employees wanting to strike back. As a matter of fact, there are even Web sites for angry employees that provide suggestions for how to stick it to the boss. Anger has many manifestations!

You may want to suggest other, more constructive ways for

Best Tip

If people are angry with you over the change, don't take it personally. Acknowledge that they have a right to be angry.

employees to express anger. Also, allow them to air their conflicting feelings. The more they emote, the faster they'll work out their anger.

Dealing with Bargaining and Depression. Engage in active listening. That means really paying attention and responding to what the employee has to say. Also, while you shouldn't argue with the employee, correct misperceptions or distortion of the truth. You want to ensure people stay based in reality. Encourage them to express what they are thinking and how they feel.

Reaching Acceptance. In this stage you want to correct any misperceptions employees may have about their particular circumstances. You want them to focus on the future by thinking about what they plan to do. Continue to support their expression of feelings. Encourage discussion about both the positive and negative effects of the change that has taken place.

Help Employees Get Back on Track

Your first concern with employees experiencing change should be for employees themselves. Do whatever you can to ensure they deal with change positively. Help them see the change as a growth experience that can be managed and, in many circumstances, used to their advantage.

To get people in a positive frame of mind, help enhance the employee's self-esteem. Here are some tips for doing just that:

1. Reinforce positive behaviors through praise, recognition, and reward.

2. Identify opportunities to give employees challenging work.

3. Involve employees in planning and decision making wherever and whenever practical.

4. Show that you care for and value your employees as people and co-workers.

As students, we all studied the Lewis and Clark Expedition. Captains Meriwether Lewis and William Clark were both exceptional leaders who understood and cared for their men. Although traversing thousands of uncharted miles through rugged wilderness, numerous Native American tribes, and untold physical dangers, they made it to the Pacific and back without the loss of a man.

Throughout their long journey they kept their men focused on a single mission: preparing for the expansion of their fledgling country to the west. Lewis and Clark involved them in making critical decisions during the trip, assigning each important roles and responsibilities. And, upon return, Lewis campaigned long and hard with the federal government to make sure that each received ample recognition and compensation for what they had endured in their epic-making journey.

The Lewis and Clark expedition is a textbook read on how to manage people through periods of dramatic change.

The Agile Manager's Lessons Learned

✔ Engage in open communication. It's the agile manager's most effective tool for managing change.

✔ Use good interpersonal communication skills. That's how you can help employees deal with loss in the workplace best.

✔ Be available to speak to an employee or an employee group at any given time or place. That's what open communication is all about.

✔ Remember: Communication can be very therapeutic, and often it's just a matter of listening.

✔ Don't be a therapist. If an employee shows signs of intense emotional or psychological upset, get professional assistance immediately.

Chapter Seven

Identify
Resistance to Change

Manuel worked quietly at the test bench, looking at the product he'd just been handed. It was from Murphy's development team. A piece of garbage, he thought. We never should've hooked up with these people. They are going to make us look bad. And I'm back to doing routine tests on products, just like I did when I interned here.

Well, he continued thinking, I know how to deal with you. He took the unit and put it in a drawer underneath the test bench. "I'll test you when I want to test you," he said aloud.

Come on now, admit it. We all resist change. No one likes it. Why? Because it disturbs the status quo. All matter seeks balance: a state of homeostasis in which all elements in a given environment are in equilibrium. There's not only elegance in such a state, but there is also tranquility, safety, and security.

And wouldn't we all want to live in such a world? As a matter of fact, all carbon-based life forms seek out such a condition. Unfortunately, as I pointed out in the beginning of this book, all life is change. Your greatest challenge is to help employees understand this universal truth and to overcome their resistance to change.

Machiavelli explains your challenge best:

> There is nothing more difficult to carry out, nor more doubtful of success, nor more dangerous to handle, than to initiate a new order of things. For the former has enemies in all who profit by the old order, and lukewarm defenders in all who would profit by the new order.

Reasons People Resist Change

While resistance to change might be genetically ingrained in us, it's greater in some than in others. That's because there are many reasons we resist change. They have to do with who we are, what we do, our relationships with others and our personal view of life, to name a few.

Here are some of the most significant reasons people resist change:

Self-interest. It's the old WAM question. What About Me? People will resist any change when that change has an effect, whether real or not, on their lives. If the change threatens their job, their responsibilities, authority, status, prestige, or paycheck, they will resist. Wouldn't you? You probably have. So resistance is understandable and natural.

Anxiety. People become anxious when they contemplate a major change. The unknown produces anxiety. They just don't know what the new environment is going to be like. The greater the unknown, the higher the state of uncertainty. The greater the

Best Tip

Understand that everyone resists change—even you, even the CEO. But we have to overcome that resistance.

uncertainty, the greater the anxiety. To decrease anxiety, people resist change in hope of returning to the status quo.

This can happen, for example, when you close a facility. A

few years back, I was part of a team that closed a hospital. Most of the people were offered new jobs in the organization or jobs with other health-care providers. Yet the vast majority of employees resisted the change. When the hospital closed, a good number remained unemployed for many months afterward. They resisted rather than move to a new job, with new co-workers, roles, and responsibilities.

> **Best Tip**
>
> Expect some employees to fight rather than switch. Many of the fighters are secretly afraid of failing in a new system.

Fear of failure. Some employees will resist a change because they fear failing in a new environment. If a production process changes, requiring a high level of proficiency in computer technology, employee technophobes may feel ill-equipped to do well in the new work environment. They'd rather fight than switch. Fighting they know, switching they need to learn, and learning can be difficult.

Differences of opinion. Sometimes employees resist because they have genuine differences of opinion with management about a proposed change. And sometimes they're right! So it behooves managers to listen and listen intently to employees when they argue against a change.

Don't assume that employees resist because they fear change. They may and often do have very legitimate concerns about a change. Give their arguments a fair hearing. If you decide to move forward with the change, explain why you believe the change is for the better. Then, recalling the words of Davy Crockett, "Be sure you're right, then go ahead."

Relationships with superiors. Many an employee has resisted a change simply because he or she has a poor relationship with the manager. After all, why would an employee support a change that might improve things and make a despised manager look good?

When poor relationships exist, it's impossible for employees to trust the manager and his judgments. It's also unlikely that the manager can depend on the unqualified support of his staff. Moreover, in such situations a sense of team rarely exists, so neither employees nor managers feel committed to the success of the other.

Lack of trust. Here I'm talking about the trust that exists between an organization and its employees. How much do employees trust in what the senior management tells them? If senior management tells you that a merger won't result in lost jobs and it does, what happens when senior management makes a similar promise? Employees won't believe it, and rightfully so. Once trust is lost it's hard to regain.

And once regained it must be zealously and jealously guarded. Too often, however, senior management fritters away its must valuable asset—its *word*. Without it, the organization is powerless to convince any of its key constituencies to support radical change initiatives.

Management may also have done a lousy job selling the change initiative. So bad, in fact, employees get the idea that you don't know what you're doing. If they don't trust your decision making, they're not going to follow you very far, if at all!

Guard well your most valuable asset—your word. Credibility must be your sword in waging a fight for change.

Status quo. This is where we began and where we end. Many of us prefer the status quo, even if we don't like it. That's because the devil you know is better than the devil you don't know. Getting people to buy into changing the status quo requires thoughtful planning.

Recognize Forms of Resistance

Briefly, those are some of the major reasons why people resist change. Resistance, however, takes many forms.

Poor performance. Poor performance comes in both passive and active forms. In a passive form, employees' performance may slip because they are extremely anxious or fearful of the change. They do whatever they can covertly to slow or prevent the change. Examples: Slowing down or failing to respond to requests.

Active resistance might involve lower productivity, sloppy work, or excessive tardiness. Poor performance may also reflect an organized effort among employees resisting the change.

Passive resistance. This type of resistance can be quite subtle but, like pornography, you'll know it when you see it. You may experience it as lack of cooperation, especially among those who are usually cooperative.

Another form of passive resistance is what I call the *monkey wrench syndrome.* You'll find employees who'll do whatever they can to foul up the change process without doing anything overt. Because of the role they play or the job they do, they can gum up the works simply by not doing something or doing it inefficiently. They might drag their feet on ordering new equipment, processing a request form, or conducting an inspection. Whatever it is, the process just doesn't seem to move along as smoothly as it once did.

Best Tip
Know that while some forms of resistance can be quite subtle, you will usually know it when you see it.

Lastly, you'll see a pulling away of some employees. Those who you'd normally expect to volunteer or actively participate in problem solving suddenly lose interest in their jobs, the department, and the organization.

Active resistance. There is nothing subtle about active resistance. You'll recognize it because it's like being slammed on the side of the head with a two-by-four. It leaves an impression.

Active resistance takes a number of forms:

Jawboning. The most common form of active resistance is jawboning. An employee engaged in jawboning will continuously berate his fellow employees with negative arguments, often very strident, about the change process. These arguments may be factual or not; it doesn't matter. It's the continuous stream of negative commentary that defines this form of resistance.

Organizing resistance. Some activist employees may become engaged in organizing active resistance. In an earlier example, I discussed closing a hospital. Shortly after announcing the closing, a small group of employees formed a "Save Our Hospital" movement that drew widespread employee, management, and community support. The movement remained active long after the hospital closed.

*B*est *T*ip
Assume that some employees will organize resistance industriously. They may gain some potent allies or even spawn an attempt to unionize.

On another occasion, when I was involved in merging two large health-care providers, a number of employees became involved in organizing a union. They saw the union as the only advocate strong enough to protect them. Unfortunately, some of your best natural leaders can also pose the greatest danger to implementing change.

Participating in organized resistance. Rather than leading organized resistance, others may opt to participate in it. The Save Our Hospital effort, for example, drew the active participation of a majority of the employees, including the hospital's former CEO.

Participation can involve attending meetings, distributing literature, participating in rallies, making telephone calls, writing letters, signing petitions or participating in the unionizing effort.

Recognizing resistance is one thing. Overcoming it is another, which we'll tackle next.

The Agile Manager's Lessons Learned

✔ Understand that the primary reason people resist change is out of self-interest. Other reasons:

—People fear that change will cause them to lose some thing of value.

—Employees don't believe there is a need for change or that the change will help.

—Many don't like the idea of change because it disrupts their lives.

✔ Understand that resistance to change comes in two forms: passive and active.

✔ Watch for poor job performance—it's a common form of resistance to change.

✔ Recognize that employees engage in passive resistance by not committing themselves to their jobs.

✔ Expect some employees to stall, stop, or undo the change. That's active resistance.

Chapter Eight

Overcome Resistance To Change

"Now," the CEO said "that's the vision. As I hope you can see, it was either a case of merge with another company on friendly terms, or be acquired by someone else in a hostile fashion. And we wanted to be in control of our own destiny.

"Also, remember that we're not going to throw this change at you and force you to conform. We've had to get the merger going, which is why we asked many of you to do things you may not have done for a while. But within each department there will soon be a change team that will have a great deal of say as to how the merger gets implemented at the operational level.

"And even if you're not on the change team, you'll have input into what happens." He paused and looked directly into the eyes of one person in the audience. "That's my pledge to you. If this promise doesn't match the reality you encounter in your departments, then e-mail me directly and I'll be in touch."

Manuel thought about the unit he'd stashed under the test bench and felt guilty. Maybe I can get to it this afternoon, he said to himself.

Understanding why people at every level of the organization

may resist change is the first step in managing the resistance. It's also the reason why many managers don't like implementing change—of any kind. It's a pain in the butt. While difficult and taxing, however, successfully implementing change in your organization may have the greatest impact on its future success.

> **Best Tip**
>
> Prepare the ground now for changes that will come later by explaining to employees the importance of meeting the challenges of the marketplace.

Yours is a heady role. In many cases, you will be both architect of, and advocate for, change. You must both plan the implementation of change as well as make the case for change. And making the case for change is the best way to prevent resistance to it.

In making the case for change, managers can be very influential. But they are often ineffective. That's because they fail to practice good communication.

Communicate the Competitive Necessity for Change

Don't wait for an impending change to start talking to your employees about why change is necessary. Start now. Employees have to understand the nature of the world economy and the competitive marketplace. They have to understand your company's position relative to its competitors. They have to know what it's going to take to be successful.

At the top of that list of success factors is implementing change. Every industry must, today, adapt to constant, technological, operational, managerial, and environmental change. The faster organizations adapt, the more likely it is that they'll gain and hold a competitive edge.

Organizations that remain competitive year in and year out have the habit of being able to introduce new products or enhanced products much more quickly than their competitors. That's because change isn't something that happens to them. It is what they do to make things happen.

In short, educate your staff about the realities of the market-place and the demand that these realities have on requiring constant change in your workplace.

Make the Case for the Change at Hand

Having prepared your employees for the need for change, the next step is making the case for changes being planned. These changes might be ordained from above or may be those you have decided to implement. Whatever the situation, you have to make the case for support to your staff.

Be aware that making the case for change that has been ordained from the top is often harder than making the case for your own change efforts. With top-down change, such as most radical change, employees rarely have the opportunity to get involved in the analysis of and planning for the change. Hence, they haven't bought into the need for the change or the plan for implementing it. With your own plan, you will ideally involve your staff in the planning.

With top-down change it's important to make the case in the context of the overall organization. For instance, when we introduced Total Quality Management (TQM) at our health-care facility, we started by first introducing managers at every level to the concept. We stressed TQM as a strategic tool, a method for improving our competitive edge. TQM would make us more responsive to patient needs, more efficient in our processes, and more quality-oriented in the services we provided.

People bought into the organizational changes that TQM would require because they saw a strategic benefit in the process. They also had been indoctrinated well in the harsh economic realities of the health-care marketplace.

The manager's task, then, is to ensure that employees understand senior management's thinking in implementing the change strategy.

The easiest way to make such a case is to provide concrete examples. Back to the TQM case: To make our point, we'd discuss a simple issue like cycle time. We'd relate it to something everyone understood, like waiting to have an X-ray taken. Your appointment was for 10 A.M., and an hour later you're still waiting. Irritating, isn't it? It may even cause you to change health providers.

Employees were made to understand how TQM addresses and improves cycle time and thus improves customer satisfaction and competitiveness in the marketplace. The more processes we improve, we explained, the more competitive we become.

When making a case for your own change initiative, it's important to have employees participate in the process. They should participate from the very beginning, starting with a needs assessment: "Do we need to improve or change this work process?" It's a lot easier making the case for a homegrown change initiative, because those who are affected by the change are also those advocating for the change. Often, employees will champion such a change because they see how it will improve their own work processes.

Ensure Employees Understand the Plan for Change

Once you've committed to implementing change, you have to plan for it. Employees have to be made aware of every aspect of the plan. They have to know what will be required of them in terms of individual roles and responsibilities, the process for monitoring and evaluating the plan, and the implementation schedule for the plan. Discuss the plan in detail with all members of your staff.

Involve Employees in the Change Initiative

Without a doubt, involving employees in the change initiative is among the most effective approaches to overcoming resistance. As mentioned earlier, engage employees in the change process from the start. Don't wait until it's a done deal.

There are a number of ways to engage employees:

- Solicit their ideas in identifying potential problems and their solutions.
- Use employees as a sounding board for testing proposed change initiatives.
- Involve employees in choosing potential changes that might be pursued.
- Identify potential change leaders among the employee group.
- Place employees on the change-initiative planning group.
- Involve employees in implementing the change.
- Make employees involved in the planning responsible for communicating with their work-team members.
- Place monitoring and control functions in the hands of employees.

Provide Support for Employees

Once employees have become committed to the change process, it's up to you to stand behind them. The manager must be responsible for ensuring that employees are properly trained for their new roles and responsibilities. You have to ensure that staff has the equipment, supplies, training, and facilities necessary to get the job done.

You must also be prepared to recognize and reward staff for the job they are doing. And don't take forever doing it, either. Sometimes, employees will confront a very difficult period during a change initiative. Know when the

Involve employees in planning the change initiative. Without a doubt, it's one of the most effective means at your disposal to overcome resistance.

time is right to say thank you and to recognize people for the sacrifices they are making.

Overcome Resistance through Negotiation

Another approach to overcoming resistance is to negotiate an agreement with employees regarding the change. You might guarantee jobs, no change in responsibilities, added bonuses, incentives, or a change in work schedules. Negotiate in good faith, and make sure you have the support and approval of senior management. Don't promise unless you can deliver.

Also, whatever the negotiated agreement, it should be fair, equitably applied, and consistent with the change process itself. For example, you can't make promises about guaranteeing jobs in your department if the change initiative increases productivity using fewer employees.

In my last job in the health care industry, I was involved in a merger of two very large organizations. Nurses at one were unionized, but not at the other.

To effect the merger, we had to negotiate for the support of both groups. As part of that negotiation we made guarantees to both. We guaranteed the nonunion nurses that they would not be forced to join the union, and that they would have the same job protections as the unionized staff.

We guaranteed the unionized nurses that we would not oppose any future efforts to organize in the new organization.

The negotiation led to the active support of the nonunion nurses and to the neutral position of the nurses union.

By successfully negotiating with both groups, the merger was able to move forward.

Ensure Employees Know There Is No Turning Back

Sometimes employees will hedge their bets. They won't commit themselves all the way because they figure, well, this thing may not work out they way they've planned. They'll lie back, planning to avoid the fallout if the change fails.

Make it crystal clear: Once the line is crossed, there is no going back. Once you've committed to a change strategy it can only be successful if everyone commits to it totally. Julius Caesar said as much when he uttered, "The die is cast. I have crossed the Rubicon." With those words he committed himself and his legions to march on Rome. It was an act of sedition. But because he and his legions were decisive and committed, they were victorious.

So disabuse anyone on your staff of the notion that you can always go back to the way you did it before. There is no going back. There is no return to the old days, the old times, the old methods. There is only change, and more change.

The Agile Manager's Lessons Learned

✔ Help employees understand why change is necessary. They'll be better able to accept it.

✔ Encourage people to understand that change isn't what happens to organizations—it's what organizations do to make things happen.

✔ Plan to educate employees about the need for change, then make the case for change.

✔ To be successful, employees must understand the plan for implementing change.

✔ Once employees commit to the change, support them fully.

✔ Consider negotiating with employees to gain their support for change.

✔ Convince employees there's no turning back. It'll help them commit to change.

Chapter Nine

Handle Stress Resulting from Change

The Agile Manager bolted upright in his bed. In his dream, he'd been making out a to-do list that had so many pages, it was the size of a notebook. He felt his forehead; it was damp.

The next day, he bumped into Wanda as he got out of his car. "What's that for," she said brightly, glancing at his athletic bag. "Wait, don't answer. First let me tell you that I really appreciate you listening to me the other day. I felt lighter afterwards. I'm still not happy about my new role, but I'll make the best of it."

"That's great," said the Agile Manager. "Remember, this is going to be a much bigger company. I think there's fresh opportunity for us all."

"I hope you're right. So what's that?" she said, again pointing at the bag.

"I've rediscovered the company fitness center," he said. "Have you tried the new elliptical trainer in there? Forty minutes on that thing is the best cure for insomnia I've ever come across."

As you've seen, adapting to change, while necessary, isn't necessarily easy. One effect of change is stress.

There are as many definitions of stress as there are books on psychology. You know it when you feel it. Imagine your boss has asked to see you. Your muscles tighten. Your stomach begins to feel queasy. Blood rushes from your head, hands and feet to your shoulder and thigh muscles. Blood pressure soars. Heart races. You begin to sweat. Your body prepares for either fight or flight. Yup, that's stress all right!

The Yin and Yang of Stress

Stress isn't all bad. As a matter of fact, some stress is even good. Researchers have shown that there is an optimal level of stress that increases our productivity. It's when our bodies are overloaded with stress that we start to suffer. Understanding when you're under too much stress and how to handle it is essential to coping with stressful situations—like constant change.

So stress, like the Chinese symbol of the *T'ai-chi T'u*—or Diagram of the Supreme Ultimate, the yin and the yang—represents both a threat and an opportunity. Stress can threaten to overwhelm us. It can hinder

Yin and Yang

both our mental and physical processes when we need them the most. With that threat comes an opportunity. If harnessed, stress can heighten our senses, and excite and motivate us.

Since stress, like change, cannot be avoided, we might as well learn how to exploit it. Learn to go with the flow, turning negative stress into positive action.

Change and Stress

Change is a natural stressor. Whenever your environment or personal situation changes, stress occurs. Psychologists tell us that there are three sources of stress. It can come from an external situation, such as a demanding job. It can be caused by thinking about something, such as worrying about losing your job. Finally, it can be related to a physical problem, such as not getting enough sleep, a poor diet, or illness.

Effects of stress on you and your employees. Stress can have both physical and emotional effects—the mind-body connection. The physical effects of stress run the gamut from headaches to neck pain and everything in between.

Best Tip

Understand that stress can cause physical effects such as back pain, dizziness, rashes, sweating, and more.

For example, many Americans suffer from one very common ailment—back pain. In large measure, back pain is either caused by or related to stress. If you can manage your stress, you can manage your back pain.

Stress not only affects your muscles but also your nervous system. It can cause dizziness, chest pain, rashes, dry mouth, sweats, diarrhea, panic attacks, and much more. We all react differently. Your physical reactions to stress are probably different from mine but they all have the same source. If not managed, stress can take a considerable toll on your body.

Just as prevalent and as dangerous are the emotional and behavioral effects of stress. Stress can cause a wide range of emotional reactions, including depression, anxiety, nervousness, nightmares, loss of appetite, difficulty in concentrating, isolation, and suicidal thoughts.

Your behavior can also change under stress. You may experience reduced productivity, lack of concern for being on time, edginess, lethargy, sleep problems, or poor eating habits. Stress can also cause you to be distracted and disorganized. Recent research has shown that acute stress causes the production of certain chemicals in the nervous system that literally turn off parts of your brain that help you concentrate.

Stress and productivity. As mentioned earlier, stress has a curvilinear relationship with productivity. Initially as stress increases, productivity increases to a point of peak performance. However, as you become overloaded with stress, productivity begins to fall rapidly. The trick is to reach the optimal level of stress. You want to be energized, not enervated.

For managers, the challenge is to exert enough demand on workers to motivate them to high levels of productivity without falling into that negative stress zone. You need to challenge your employees, not threaten them.

It's like coaching a football team. You need to push them to the point of peak physical and emotional performance without over-training or over-preparing them. How often have very good teams been blown off the field come Sunday simply because they peaked too early, entering the game physically and emotionally spent?

Stress and resistance to change. Most of us don't mind having some stress in our lives. We intuitively understand that it's necessary to keep us excited, motivated, alive. After all, it would be a dull world without it. But when stress overloads and overwhelms us, we react by either fighting against it or fleeing from it.

Our bodies and our minds can take only so much physical and emotional abuse before they react and react strongly. We either look for ways to avoid the stressor causing the discomfort or we try to eliminate it. The many ways we resist change in the workplace are merely our attempts to save ourselves from the constant ravages of negative stress on our bodies and our psyches.

COPE WITH STRESS

Whether good stress or bad stress, you can manage it. Coping requires you to learn how to reduce or master stress.

Let's discuss some approaches that you can use to manage your own stress, as well as how you can assist your employees in managing their stress.

Managing Your Own Stress

Here are my baker's dozen methods to managing stress in your life.

Listen to your body. If you're suffering from any of the physical symptoms discussed earlier, then you know it's time to start managing your stress. Don't wait until you develop a severe physical problem before addressing your stress.

Exercise. This is my number one favorite method for dealing with stress.

To me, there are two general philosophies for dealing with stress—Eastern and Western. Eastern philosophy relies on a Zen approach: Embrace the stress, go with the flow, get in touch with your inner self. By the way, this approach works.

On the other hand, the Western approach, my preference, is to beat the crap out of the stress by attacking it through exercise. Run it to death. Pump iron. Do aerobics. Vigorous exercise strengthens the body and energizes the immune system. It also gets those endorphins running around your cerebellum, creating a positive mindset.

Meditate. This is a great way to lessen both the physical and emotional effects of stress. Twenty minutes a day meditating can have a very positive effect. It can lower blood pressure, reduce feelings of anxiety, and bring about a feeling of peace and contentment. It's also a great way to escape from the cares of the world, if only for a few minutes. By combining meditation with physical exercise, you double your pleasure and relief. Try it!

Organize your time. Often we create or add to our stress by misusing our time. Schedule your most important work during the time of day when you are most productive. Develop a daily "hit list" of things to do and prioritize them. Ensure that each item on your list is directly related to helping you accomplish specific personal or work goals and objectives.

Leave your work at the office. Don't take your work home—at least not on a regular basis. It not only disrupts your family life—and there's too much disruption already—but it also steals precious "down" time from you. We all need to get away, to reenergize our batteries. The home should be a quiet, safe haven from the cares of the world. Do not let work intrude into your peaceful space.

Develop outside interests and hobbies. The life that is circumscribed by one's work is no life at all. Develop a wide range of interests and at least one hobby or avocation. I suggest one, because your goal is to become accomplished at it. Painting, photography, wood carving, writing, golf—it doesn't matter. You'll find it a great source of comfort and pleasure throughout your life, not to mention a great stress reliever.

Develop a relationship with your superiors. No, it doesn't have to be social. But you should work to develop mutual understanding and respect between you and your superiors. Communicate with them frequently. Let them know what you're doing, your accomplishments, and your plans for the future. By building strong relationships, you're in a better position to call on their support when needed.

Carve out time for one significant hobby or avocation, like golf or model building. It'll help keep you sane.

Avoid negative co-workers. Surround yourself with positive, bright, and supportive peers. There is enough negativism in the world without importing it into your professional circle. Negative individuals suck the lifeblood out of everyone around them. Avoid them. Choose to associate with peers who want you to succeed and who build you up rather than tear you down.

Acquire new skills. Never let pass an opportunity to acquire new skills. A new skill can enhance your job performance, create promotion opportunities, or open up a whole new career path. Take advantage of them.

Consider looking for another job. Sometimes fleeing a stressful job situation is the best strategy. Looking for a new job can be exciting as well as a great morale booster. It's nice to know that there are other organizations out there who value you and your set of skills, and who are willing to pay for it.

Do not be afraid to seek help. If you're really stressed out, seek professional counsel. You can use your employee assistance program or a private counselor. Sometimes we need professional guidance to help us understand and manage stress. Seeking professional counseling is not a sign of weakness. It's a sign of maturity.

Identify a friend or ally. Find that person whom you can confide in, someone who doesn't make judgments about you or your job, and someone who is supportive and willing to listen whenever you want to talk. We all need that special someone. It can be a spouse, longtime friend, family member, or co-worker.

Women tend to be better at identifying and cultivating such relationships than men. So men, take your lead from women and learn how to develop trusting, supportive relationships. It will pay innumerable dividends.

Pay attention to your career. A good career will sustain you in times of difficulty and trouble. Your career is something that belongs only to you, no one else. Nurture it. Protect it. Work at it.

Help Your People Manage Stress

Naturally, your employees can use all of the above techniques. In addition, there are some other approaches that you can use to help your employees to cope with stress.

Encourage employees to focus on their immediate tasks. As noted, stress can cause employees to be distracted and confused about what tasks should take priority. Help them prioritize tasks. Identify the major objectives and goals of the department and how each task relates to accomplishing those objectives and goals. Also, remind them of what their principal roles and responsibilities are so that they can put their work tasks in context. Keep them focused on the job at hand.

Involve them in planning and implementing the change

initiative. When you involve employees in planning the change initiative, you give them some degree of control over the change. With control, employees feel less threatened. Since they are helping to plan the change, they are more knowledgeable about the change. This reduces the level of uncertainty and results in less anxiety, further reducing the stress.

The same can be said for implementation. All of us are far more enthusiastic about implementing a change that we've helped plan. Having planned the change, employees are also better prepared to deal with the stress caused by the change.

Best **Tip**
Don't be afraid to discuss stress-related problems with your employees. Just talking can help relieve them.

Encourage employees to take time off. The great failure in American work life is our reluctance to use our vacation time. How many of us have left a job with weeks or even months of accrued vacation time? It isn't that we have passion for our jobs as much as we fear losing those jobs. Encourage employees to use their vacation time to get away, far away from the maddening workplace. If necessary, require it!

Discuss issues of stress openly. Talk to your staff about stress and how to cope with it. Bring the issue out in the open, especially if it is having an effect on your workforce. Share ideas for addressing stress. Also, be sure people know that you're available to talk with them, and make sure they know how to access professional help if they need it.

Be supportive. If an employee is showing signs of stress, be both supportive and understanding. Serve as a confidant. Examine options to reduce stress, such as changes in work schedule, responsibilities, or demands made of the employee. Be available if anyone needs you.

Have a sense of humor. Be able to laugh at yourself and to laugh with your employees about life in general and work in particular. Humor provides a perspective on us and our work life that is insightful and therapeutic. Those who laugh together usually work well together, mainly because they see the world through the same prism. And when possible, have a little fun in the workplace.

Develop Stress Hardiness

Psychologists refer to an individual's general ability to adapt to change as stress resistance or stress hardiness. So an employee who is stress hardy would see the reengineering of her production line as a challenge, not a threat. She would view the loss of a job not as a catastrophe but as an opportunity to look for a more challenging position. That's good mental health as well as stress hardiness.

Some are born stress resistant, while others have to develop it. With employees, stress hardiness requires developing a sense of control combined with an openness to change and a feeling of empowerment.

Control. I've said this before and I'll say it again: The greater the control, the less the stress. People who feel they are in control feel they can master any situation. With that mindset they may feel challenged by change but rarely threatened by it.

As you've seen, one way to give employees control, or at least some degree of control, is to have them participate in the planning and implementation of the change initiative. The more people feel in control of the change, the less likely it is that they will feel threatened by the change or inordinately stressed by the change.

Openness to change. By definition, those open to change are stress hardy. Managers can help employees open themselves to change by first giving them some control over the change, as discussed above. Second, they can stress (excuse the pun) how the change will benefit them, as well as the organization. Third, they can use the change to motivate employees by offering incentives and rewards for successful implementation. And lastly, they can excite employees with the prospect of new and challenging work.

Empowering employees. With control, employees become empowered. Employees, remember, are empowered when they are put in control of their work processes. Part of controlling your own work is to continuously adjust or change the process to maintain or improve its performance.

When empowered, employees become accustomed to constant change, forever tinkering and adjusting their processes to work at peak performance. They come not to resist change but to exploit it.

The Agile Manager's Lessons Learned

✔ Remember: Change can both threaten and challenge. It can cause stress, some of it good and some of it bad.

✔ Because the physical and emotional effects of change can be destructive, plan to deal with stress—both yours and that of your employees.

✔ Manage your stress. Doing that begins with listening to your body.

✔ To reduce stress, let employees participate in planning and implementing the change.

✔ Develop stress hardiness. It's the most effective approach for coping with change.

✔ Maintain a sense of control—it's the first step in developing stress hardiness.

*E*pilogue:
One Last Time

You, the manager, play an intrinsic and essential role in managing organizational change:

- As leader, you provide focus and direction.
- As educator, you provide knowledge and perspective.
- As coach, you provide skills and competence.
- As motivator, you provide encouragement and discipline.
- And as mentor, you provide guidance and counsel.

The demands on you are great, but so are the rewards. Your ability to manage change will be reflected in both the success of your employees and your organization. View change as a unique opportunity to make that success happen!

Final Thoughts on Managing Change

For those who want to cut to the chase and read the last chapter first—or for those of you who want a recap—turn the page for a brief summation of everything I've said about managing change.

1. Change is both inevitable and necessary—learn to live with it, deal with it, manage it.

2. All successful change management begins with effective leadership both at the strategic and operational level.

3. The first step in managing change is identifying the need for change.

4. Successfully implementing radical change begins with convincing those affected that the change is necessary.

5. All change, whether routine or radical, results in loss. Some of it is significant, some of it not so.

6. When we suffer a loss, we grieve. The grieving process may be brief or long. But it is a process that we must pass through if we are to move on in accepting and managing change in our lives.

7. Communicating openly and candidly is the first step in assisting employees with the grieving process.

8. Building and maintaining employee self-esteem is the most effective method for assisting employees in overcoming work-related loss and returning to the workplace as effective and productive members of the work team.

9. People resist change for many reasons but it all begins with self-interest.

10. The first question that people want answered in the face of impending change is, "What About Me?"

11. The first step in overcoming resistance to change is to make a compelling case for the need for change.

12. As a natural consequence of change, stress can be both constructive and destructive.

13. To develop stress hardiness among employees begin by giving them a sense of control over their work environment.

14. Successful organizations, managers and employees see themselves not as victims of change but as masters of change.

Index